NEW DIRECTIONS FOR TEACHING AND LEARNING

Student Ratings of Instruction: Issues for Improving Practice

Michael Theall, Jennifer Franklin

EDITORS

NUMBER 43, FALL 1990
JOSSEY-BASS INC., PUBLISHERS

NEW DIRECTIONS FOR TEACHING AND LEARNING

Robert E. Young, *University of Wisconsin*
EDITOR-IN-CHIEF

Student Ratings of Instruction: Issues for Improving Practice

Michael Theall
University of Alabama

Jennifer Franklin
Northeastern University

EDITORS

Number 43, Fall 1990

JOSSEY-BASS INC., PUBLISHERS
San Francisco

941918

STUDENT RATINGS OF INSTRUCTION: ISSUES FOR IMPROVING PRACTICE
Michael Theall, Jennifer Franklin (eds.)
New Directions for Teaching and Learning, no. 43
Robert E. Young, Editor-in-Chief

Microfilm copies of issues and articles are available in 16mm and 35mm,
as well as microfiche in 105mm, through University Microfilms Inc., 300
North Zeeb Road, Ann Arbor, Michigan 48106.

LC 85-644763   ISSN 0271-0633   ISBN 1-55542-817-7

NEW DIRECTIONS FOR TEACHING AND LEARNING is part of The Jossey-
Bass Higher and Adult Education Series and is published quarterly by
Jossey-Bass Inc., Publishers. Second-class postage paid at San Francisco,
California, and at additional mailing offices. Postmaster: Send address
changes to Jossey-Bass Inc., Publishers, 350 Sansome Street, San Fran-
cisco, California 94104.

EDITORIAL CORRESPONDENCE should be sent to Jossey-Bass Inc., Publishers, 350 Sansome Street, San Francisco, California 94104.

Cover photograph by Richard Blair/Color & Light © 1990.

Printed on acid-free paper in the United States of America.

CONTENTS

EDITORS' NOTES

The evaluation of teaching, especially through the use of student ratings, is a topic that generates comment, controversy, and confusion. At professional meetings, in print, in faculty senate debates, and in private discussions, the validity and reliability of student raters continue to be major issues.

It is unfortunate that so much of this discussion is not informed by the consistent results of over three decades of research: that students' opinions can provide important information, and that valid questions, answered by students in the context of appropriate data-collection processes, will yield reliable and useful results. When student raters are used, they typically provide the following information:

- Opinions or estimates (when asked, for example, to note the frequency of certain behaviors on the part of teachers, or to assess the difficulty or workload of a course)
- The value they place on their experiences (when, for example, they are asked to rate the importance of what they have learned in a course)
- Summary opinions (when they are asked to compare the performance of one instructor to that of another: "Compare this instructor's performance to that of other college instructors you have had").

But are students actually the evaluators? While giving responses on ratings forms is, generally speaking, a way of evaluating, the student's role stops short of the commonly accepted goal of evaluation: making a decision about merit or worth. When the role of evaluation is formative (as in course improvement), decision makers may be faculty members, curriculum developers, instructional designers, or others, but the debate does not center on formative decision making; it is the use of student ratings in promotion, tenure, and merit decisions that gives rise to anxiety, uncertainty, and hostility. This summative role of evaluation goes beyond determinations of value and into the realm of an essentially public assignment of rewards on the basis of these determinations.

We feel that the debate over student "evaluators" misses the point. In fact, even the literature on student ratings has focused mainly on issues of measurement, with particular emphasis on establishing the validity and

---

The contributors to this volume are members of the Special Interest Group in Faculty Evaluation and Development (SIGFED) of the American Educational Research Association (AERA). SIGFED actively supports scholarship and the dissemination of information on issues related to faculty evaluation and development.

reliability of student raters and with far less attention to the systematic issues of collecting, reporting, interpreting, and using evaluation results.

Who does make summative decisions? Faculty (as members of committees on promotion and tenure), department chairs, deans, provosts, and presidents do. Because they make the decisions, it is much more correct to say that they are the real evaluators. The question of import now changes its focus, from the validity and reliability of student providers of evaluative information to the validity and reliability of the use of evaluative data by faculty and administrators. There is little research investigating this question, and what little exists leads to some troubling conclusions, particularly when we recall two recent findings: that department chairs are the prime source of personnel decision making, and that student ratings are the most frequently used source of information about teaching performance.

In the areas of salary equity, systems for determining rewards, and the faculty's and administrators' attitudes and knowledge concerning evaluation, serious questions arise about the validity and reliability of administrative decisions that are based on ratings. Our own research on this issue has focused on the knowledge and attitudes of ratings users, and we have reached the unavoidable conclusion that a large percentage of those who make promotion, tenure, and merit decisions may be uninformed about or may disregard basic, crucial evaluation procedures and measurement issues. Thus, they may not distinguish appropriate from inappropriate data and may not correctly interpret the results of student ratings, even when these are reliable and valid. Further, we have found a significant positive correlation between the knowledge and the attitudes of decision makers. For example, those who do not consider students to be valid raters of instruction often respond incorrectly to questions about interpretation that require basic statistical knowledge. The consensus of many researchers and writers who are interested in the evaluation and improvement of teaching is that some new directions for research and practice are clearly needed.

This volume of *New Directions for Teaching and Learning* is concerned with collecting, reporting, interpreting, and using student ratings, with particular emphasis on issues for improving practice. We intend to provide useful information for the "real" evaluators—namely, faculty, administrators, and teaching-improvement practitioners—who make decisions at least partly on the basis of ratings data.

This volume is divided into three parts. Part One sets the scene for student ratings by providing a perspective on teaching effectiveness—that is, by discussing teaching itself. John A. Centra and Peggy Bonesteel address the evaluability of the "art or science" of teaching, and we describe the contexts in which evaluation takes place and their influence on both the processes and the use of ratings results. Part Two presents perspectives on ratings practice. Raoul A. Arreola and Lawrence M. Aleamoni review important practical considerations that must be faced in the development and implementation of systems for collecting and using student ratings. Philip McKnight views ratings from a problem-solving perspective, discussing the complex nature of evaluation and the reasons why evaluative decisions must be made so carefully. John C. Ory presents nine scenarios that describe ethical problems encountered in evaluation practice. Our own contribution to this section provides detailed information about communicating ratings results to decision makers. Part Three takes a research perspective, addressing current issues of importance in the interpretation and use of ratings. Philip C. Abrami and Sylvia d'Apollonia discuss the dimensionality and the usefulness of ratings from these various dimensions in personnel decisions; William E. Cashin reports how ratings differ across disciplines and how these differences may affect decision making. Peter A. Cohen offers insights into the ways in which bridges between research and practice can be built, stressing the importance of making effective use of ratings data, as well as of uncovering and addressing the sources of resistance to ratings.

While each chapter is useful in its own right, the connections among chapters, as well as the gestalt that results from their synthesis, are perhaps more important. That the sections and chapters are so strongly interrelated reflects not only the complexity of student ratings and evaluation but also the complexity of teaching and learning in higher education, as well as the fact that evaluation is a human endeavor, carried out in a specialized environment and affecting people who have a great investment in their own professional lives. The first two chapters provide insight into the complexities of teaching and its evaluation. The practical considerations outlined by Arreola and Aleamoni will begin to answer the questions raised by Ory and by McKnight; the research perspectives of Cohen, of Abrami and d'Apollonia, and of Cashin will reinforce one another and underscore the importance of the careful and detailed approach that we outline for communicating results to users.

Anxiety over the evaluation of one's own performance will not go away, but anxiety need not be compounded by the suspicion and hostility that arise when people perceive that decisions are made in the absence of clear and fair policy, or that data are misused, misinterpreted, or ignored. Evaluations of teaching, as well as decisions about faculty careers, are too important to be disregarded by being left to the assumption that those who make these decisions are somehow immediately qualified to do so simply by virtue of having the responsibility thrust upon them. These evaluators often need assistance. The least that can be offered to them, and to those whose performance they review, is valid, useful information and help in using it efficiently and accurately. Student ratings can provide part of the information needed for evaluative decisions. The quality of ratings data should be closely monitored, and research should continue to establish the most effective ways of collecting and presenting such data. We owe one another and our students no less than an equivalent effort, to ensure that student-ratings practice is well informed and that evaluation data are properly used.

Michael Theall
Jennifer Franklin
Editors

Michael Theall is associate professor and director of the Center for Teaching and Learning at the School of Education, University of Alabama, Birmingham.

Jennifer Franklin is senior research associate at the Center for Applied Social Research and manager of the Office of Instructional Evaluation at Northeastern University.

PART ONE

Perspectives on Teaching
and Evaluating

Is college teaching an art or a science? No matter what the answer, teachers and teaching must still be evaluated.

College Teaching: An Art or a Science?

John A. Centra, Peggy Bonesteel

In his well-known book *The Art of Teaching,* Highet (1959) argues that teaching is an art, not a science. Teaching, he proposes, involves emotions that cannot be systematically appraised and employed; moreover, a "scientific relationship between humans, whether it be in teaching, marriage or friendship, will be inadequate and as cold as a chess problem" (p. vii). For Highet, teaching is more like painting a picture or composing music.

Is teaching an art? Does good teaching require the creative skill that good art requires? Is a person born with the skills to be a good teacher, skills that may be somewhat personal and uncovered only through practice? If so, then it is unlikely that we can do very much to develop teachers or systematically assess performance in teaching. Whether teaching is solely an art and whether good teaching can be prescribed are not trivial questions. In fact, they form the cornerstone for evaluating and improving what teachers do.

In this chapter, we propose that knowledge acquired about college teaching through careful observation and study over the years has provided a basis for classifying teaching as at least as much a science as an art. Studies have identified attributes related to good teaching. This is not to say that no room is left for variations on principles or for individual expression. Teachers are not computers. Creativity, individuality, and other human qualities are important features that are integral components of good teaching. Gage (1978) sees teaching as a practical art that calls for "intuition, creativity, improvisation, and expressiveness"; as such, it leaves room for "departure from rules, formulas, and algorithms" (p. 15). We will return to this point later.

Qualities of Good Teaching

Although he proclaims teaching to be an art, Highet (1959) goes on to describe the qualities and abilities necessary for good teaching. The qualities he includes are knowledge of one's subject, a sense of humor, and enjoyment of students. Good teachers, Highet adds, should possess certain abilities, such as memory and willpower. Highet even specifies crucial methods for good teaching—preparing course and class outlines, or finding other ways of providing structure for a course. Many of these abilities and methods are apparently subject to observation and evaluation and seem to be teachable in themselves. As such, they may be less like art than Highet claims.

Other characteristics of good teaching are similarly open to evaluation and study. A syntheses of thirty-one studies in which students and faculty members specified the characteristics important to good teaching revealed extensive similarities across studies, as well as between the two groups (Feldman, 1988). In these studies, students and faculty members at the same institutions (two-year and four-year colleges) were asked to describe attitudes or practices important to good teaching. Some studies asked respondents to characterize "best" or "ideal" teachers. Students and faculty members gave high rankings to the following factors:

- The teacher's sensitivity to and concern with class level and progress
- The teacher's preparation and organization of the course
- The teacher's knowledge of the subject
- The teacher's enthusiasm (for the subject or for teaching)
- The teacher's clarity and understandableness
- The teacher's availability and helpfulness
- The teacher's fairness
- Impartiality of the teacher's evaluation of students
- The quality of examinations.

Students in these studies placed somewhat more emphasis than faculty did on teachers' stimulation of interest and on elocutionary skills. Faculty gave more importance than students did to teachers' being intellectually challenging, encouraging independent thought, and motivating students to do their best. Both groups also mentioned the teacher's concern and respect for students; the nature and value of course material; the quality and frequency of feedback to students; and the teacher's openness to opinions of others, along with his or her encouragement of questions and discussion. All in all, the studies synthesized by Feldman indicate that faculty and students were very similar in their views of what constitutes good teaching, although differences in the relative importance of a few characteristics were evident (see also Marques, Lane, and Dorfman, 1979).

Other reviews of studies have focused on fewer characteristics of excellence in teaching, agreed on by students and faculty alike. Sherman and others (1987) identify the following five characteristics, along with selected definitions provided from various studies:

1. Enthusiasm (vocal delivery that is lively and varied; high energy level; pleasure in teaching; love of the subject; deep interest in the subject)
2. Clarity (clear explanation of concepts; comprehensibility; summarizing of major premises; systematic presentation of material)
3. Preparation and organization (detailed course outlines; establishment of course objectives; preparation for each class session; definition of evaluation procedures)
4. Stimulation (creation of interest and thoughtfulness in students; inspiration of intellectual curiosity in students; ability to be interesting, motivating, thought-provoking)
5. Knowledge (grasp of subject matter; ability to make interrelationships of knowledge areas clear).

Lowman (1984) has proposed a two-dimensional model of effective college teaching. The first dimension is what he terms "intellectual excitement," and it includes both what is taught (clarity of communication) and how it is taught (public-speaking virtuosity). Skills necessary for clear communication include mastery and accuracy of content; the ability to analyze, integrate, apply, and evaluate information; and the ability to organize the subject matter. Public-speaking virtuosity includes what Lowman calls "teacher as performer" skills—the ability to use voice, gestures, and movement to stimulate emotions; a strong sense of timing; and the ability to focus energy into a teaching performance. Lowman calls the second dimension "interpersonal rapport." This dimension encompasses the teacher's awareness of interpersonal phenomena and of the communication skills that increase students' motivation, enjoyment, and independent learning. According to Lowman's model, a teacher with a high level of interpersonal rapport is extremely warm and open and exhibits predictable student-centered behavior. This teacher encourages students' questions and viewpoints, is sensitive to how students feel about the material or its presentation, and encourages students to be creative and independent in dealing with the material. By contrast, the teacher with a low level of interpersonal rapport is cold and distant, highly controlling, and possibly unpredictable. He or she shows little interest in the students as people, is openly disdainful of the students' level of performance in the course or of their nonacademic interests, seems irritated or rushed when students ask questions, and dictates requirements and policies, often becoming defensive if these are questioned. According to Lowman, outstanding teachers must excel in one or both of the model's two dimensions and be at least competent in the other. The master teacher is one whose content presentation is extremely clear and exciting and whose interpersonal relationships with students are marked by warmth, openness, predictability, and student-centeredness.

Many other studies have also gone beyond broad categories, to include specific statements that help describe each characteristic of good teaching. For example, Bridges, Ware, Brown, and Greenwood (1971) asked students, faculty members, and administrators to describe outstanding characteristics of the best and worst teachers they had known. Under the category termed "preparation and organization," respondents said that the best teachers carefully planned classes, presented outlines or syllabi to students, and provided logical organization for material. The worst teachers were random and disorganized, talked extemporaneously, and were ill prepared.

Hildebrand (1973) and Wotruba and Wright (1975) have also conducted studies to identify the specific skills or characteristics (sometimes referred to as *low-inference items*) that effective teachers possess or exhibit in their teaching. They used this information to develop instruments to collect students' ratings of instruction. Because students may not be the best respondents for assessing all aspects of teaching, researchers have also identified certain characteristics that others (say, colleagues) may be more able to assess. In short, widely acknowledged characteristics of good (and bad) teaching have become the basis for the evaluation of teaching. With student evaluators in particular, however, the question becomes not only what the characteristics of good teaching may be but which characteristics students are able to judge. Opinion surveys and analyses of students' responses have been used to select appropriate questions for students (see Wotruba and Wright, 1975; Centra, 1971).

Evaluating the Characteristics of Good Teaching

An example of how the various characteristics of good teaching can be systematically evaluated by different groups is provided in a recent monograph developed at Syracuse University (Centra, Froh, Gray, and Lambert, 1987). After selecting, from previous studies, the general characteristics to be evaluated, the Syracuse group named seven ways in which the data could be collected and six individuals or groups who could do the evaluating. The seven methods were self-assessments or self-reports, classroom observation, structured interviews, instructional rating surveys, tests or appraisals of students' achievement, content analysis of instructional materials, and review of classroom records. The data produced through these methods could be evaluated by the instructor, students, other faculty, deans or department chairs, alumni, and other appropriate administrators.

For the characteristic "good organization of subject matter and course," for example, faculty could observe a colleague's classes to judge whether the teacher had made a clear statement about the purpose of the lesson and whether major points of the lesson had been summarized. Student evaluators could be asked to judge this same characteristic by responding to questions about the extent to which the instructor was prepared for class and had presented topics logically. A department chair or another qualified person could do a content analysis of the course syllabus.

Each of these methods and evaluation sources has advantages and disadvantages. The advantages and disadvantages of the various approaches underscore not only the complexity of making evaluations but also the complexity of teaching itself. Consider, for example, the following advantages and disadvantages of classroom observation by colleagues.

Advantages. Classroom observation helps us draw a more concrete, real picture of an instructor than we usually can with the use of indirect methods, such as students' ratings and administrators' comments. Sometimes student ratings can be inconsistent for controversial instructors or situations, and classroom observation can provide information about these ratings. Classroom observation also allows a more extensive focus on substantive issues of course content, such as relevance, the instructor's knowledge of the subject, the instructor's scholarship, and integration of topics.

Disadvantages. Classroom observation has several disadvantages. First, faculty tend to find classroom observation threatening when they have never used it before. As a result, this method demands considerable tact, respect, and rapport among faculty. Second, it requires a considerable amount of faculty's time to ensure the number of observations necessary for reliable and valid conclusions. Third, observations for personnel decisions must be kept separate from observations for instructional improvement, to protect the use of this technique for either purpose. Fourth, observers tend to vary in their definitions of effective instruction, and so it is difficult for observers to reach consensus. The training of observers is therefore recommended.

Teaching is more complicated than any list of the qualities or characteristics of good teaching can suggest. The Syracuse group, writing particularly for department chairs and members of committees on tenure and promotion, discussed several caveats. First, some of these characteristics are more easily measured than others and so may get more weight than they deserve. Second, teachers display different patterns of strength, and a good teacher may be strong in many of the identified characteristics but not necessarily in all of them. The ultimate outcome of good teaching—good learning—can be achieved through a variety of approaches. For example, one teacher may not organize the course or each class session as well as one may hope, but his or her motivational skills, enthusiasm, communication skills, positive attitudes toward students, or other characteristics may more than make up for this deficiency. Lowman (1984) makes a similar point with his two-dimensional model.

Other Conceptions of Teaching

Various studies have supported the thesis that effective teaching may vary, not only according to individual style but also, to some extent, according to academic discipline and level of teaching. Effective graduate teaching, for example, is not necessarily the same as effective undergraduate teaching. Murray (1985) compared the student-ratings data on teachers who were teaching both graduate and undergraduate courses and obtained generally low correlations, a finding that indicates that teachers who do well at one level do not necessarily do well at the other.

In his study of college humanities teachers, Axelrod (1970) identifies two types of subject matter–centered instructors, two types of student-centered instructors, and a third category of instructors, which he finds to be the most common one in the humanities: instructor-centered instructors. One type of subject matter specialist believes that the teacher's task is to cover a well-defined set of topics for a course systematically and precisely, while the student's task is to master the course content through traditional assignments and study methods. Instructor-centered teachers prefer to put their own interpretations on the subject matter and are therefore more intellectual and individualistic in selecting both what to cover and how it will be covered. Student-centered teachers, probably the least common, are primarily concerned with the cognitive or personal development of students. They use analysis, problem-solving techniques, and other nontraditional methods to teach students how to approach and understand the material.

Student-centered teaching is the foundation of Katz's (1985) approach to effective teaching. He argues that teachers should make students an object of study and should engage them in collaborative efforts toward learning. According to Katz, teachers need to recognize differences in students' thinking styles, affect, motivation, and aspirations. To acquire this information, teachers need to interview students in depth and then design instruction around small-group or individualized activities. Such an approach to teaching would probably require skills that many college teachers do not yet possess, as well as a considerable commitment of time, particularly in large classes.

Innovative examples of subject matter–centered approaches are the Keller Plan, the audiotutorial method, and computer-based instruction. All three emphasize students' mastery of predetermined subject matter (even though the student is an active learner), and all three see the teacher's role as that of a developer of materials and facilitator of learning. Meta-analysis of many studies of these three methods has generally supported the positive effects of these methods on short-term achievement, particularly in the case of the Keller Plan (Kulik, Kulik, and Cohen, 1979a, 1979b, 1980). Nevertheless, the effectiveness of the teacher using these methods must not be judged in the same way that effectiveness is evaluated when traditional teaching methods have been used. In general, good teachers do a good job of organizing and presenting course material in nontraditional modes, and they supplement these methods when they need to (for example, to arouse students' interest in the subject matter).

The Scientific Basis of Teaching

So far, we have shown that there is strong consensus among and within various groups on the characteristics of effective teaching. This finding in itself does not, of course, establish teaching as a science. Does teaching have a scientific basis?

Gage (1978) argues that there is a *scientific* basis for the *art* of teaching. A science of teaching, according to Gage, requires rigorous laws that yield predictability and control. Research on teaching at the elementary and secondary levels (which Gage largely draws on to reach his conclusion) has not demonstrated attainment of such predictability. Because of the complexity of teaching, "any singly significant variable in teacher behavior should have only a low correlation (ranging from ± .1 to about ± .4) with student achievement or attitude" (Gage, 1978, p. 26). The same can be said of the characteristics of college teachers, which correlate in a similar range with course achievement when student ratings are used to assess or describe instructional variables (Centra, 1977; Cohen, 1981).

Gage (1978) and Dunkin and Barnes (1986) describe four classes of variables that have been used in research on teaching: presage variables (age, sex, social class, background, training, experience); context variables (grade level, subject matter, class size); process variables (the ways in which teachers and students behave and interact); and product or outcome variables (the extent of learning and achievement of educational objectives). In their review of research on teaching in higher education, Dunkin and Barnes (1986) conclude that the vast majority of research at the college level has been conducted with process and product variables, and much of the process part, unfortunately, has been obtained on the basis of prescriptive definitions or ratings from untrained observers, rather than on the basis of careful observation. We not only need alternative ways to document process variables, we also need to do more work with presage, context, and product variables.

In research on teaching, it is apparent that the laws or theories relating any two variables need to be modified to include other variables as well. These interactions do not occur only in research on teaching; they also appear in the natural sciences when real-life rather than laboratory phenomena are studied (Gage, 1978). Therefore, the fact that research on teaching has not produced highly predictable results does not in itself negate the scientific basis of teaching. Other practical fields and professions besides teaching also have scientific bases but require artistry to reach their desired ends. Gage mentions medicine and engineering as examples, for practice in both fields requires knowledge of much science: "Artistry enters into knowing when to follow the implications of the laws, generalizations, and trends, and especially, when *not* to, and how to combine two or more laws or trends in solving a problem" (Gage, 1978, p. 18). It seems that college teachers need to be aware not only of the scientific basis of teaching but also of when and how to build on that basis.

What does this mean for the evaluation of teaching? For one thing, evaluators and decision makers should not expect the level of precision that would perhaps be obtained if flexibility and creativity were not parts of teaching. The expectation that evaluation can result in exact rankings of groups of teachers, from good to poor, is unrealistic, and efforts in that direction will stifle the artistry that is part of teaching. Nevertheless, the evaluation techniques currently available can at least yield broader classifications of effectiveness and aid in the improvement of college teaching. Evaluation methods are ultimately subjective. Only through convergence of methods do we attain the level of validity that we need even for broad judgments.

References

Axelrod, J. "Teaching Styles in the Humanities." In W. H. Morris (ed.), *Effective College Teaching*. Washington, D.C.: American Association of Higher Education, 1970.

Bridges, C. M., Ware, W. B., Brown, B. B., and Greenwood, G. "Characteristics of the Best and Worst College Teachers." *Science Education*, 1971, 55, 545–553.

Centra, J. A. *Student Instructional Report: Its Development and Uses*. Princeton, N.J.: Educational Testing Service, 1971.

Centra, J. A. "Student Ratings of Teaching and Their Relationship to Student Learning." *American Educational Research Journal*, 1977, 14, 17–24.

Centra, J. A., Froh, R. C., Gray, P. J., and Lambert, L. M. *A Guide to Evaluating Teaching for Promotion and Tenure*. Syracuse, N.Y.: Syracuse University Center for Instructional Development, 1987.

Cohen, P. A. "Student Ratings of Instruction and Student Achievement: A Meta-Analysis of Multisection Validity Studies." *Review of Educational Research*, 1981, 51, 281–309.

Dunkin, M. J., and Barnes, J. "Research on Teaching in Higher Education." In M. C. Wittrock (ed.), *Handbook of Research on Teaching*. (3rd ed.) New York: Macmillan, 1986.

Feldman, K. A. "Effective College Teaching from the Students' and Faculty's View: Matched or Mismatched Priorities?" *Research in Higher Education*, 1988, 28, 291–344.

Gage, N. L. *The Scientific Basis of the Art of Teaching*. New York: Teachers College Press, 1978.

Highet, G. *The Art of Teaching.* New York: Vintage Books, 1959.

Hildebrand, M. "The Character and Skills of the Effective Professor." *Journal of Higher Education,* 1973, *44,* 41–50.

Katz, J. "Teaching Based on Knowledge of Students." In J. Katz (ed.), *Teaching as Though Students Mattered.* New Directions for Teaching and Learning, no. 21. San Francisco: Jossey-Bass, 1985.

Kulik, J. A., Kulik, C. L., and Cohen, P. A. "A Meta-Analysis of Outcome Studies of Keller's Personalized System of Instruction." *American Psychologist,* 1979a, *34,* 307–318.

Kulik, J. A., Kulik, C. L., and Cohen, P. A. "Research on Audiotutorial Instruction: A Meta-Analysis of Comparative Studies." *Research in Higher Education,* 1979b, *11,* 321–341.

Kulik, J. A., Kulik, C. L., and Cohen, P. A. "Effectiveness of Computer-Based College Teaching: A Meta-Analysis of Findings." *Review of Educational Research,* 1980, *50,* 525–544.

Lowman, J. *Mastering the Techniques of Teaching.* San Francisco: Jossey-Bass, 1984.

Marques, T. E., Lane, D. M., and Dorfman, P. W. "Toward the Development of a System for Instructional Evaluation: Is There Consensus Regarding What Constitutes Effective Teaching?" *Journal of Educational Psychology,* 1979, *71,* 840–849.

Murray, H. G. "Classroom Teaching Behaviors Related to College Teaching Effectiveness." In J. G. Donald and A. M. Sullivan (eds.), *Using Research to Improve Teaching.* New Directions for Teaching and Learning, no. 23. San Francisco: Jossey-Bass, 1985.

Sherman, T. M., Armistead, L. P., Fowler, F., Barksdale, M. A., and Reif, G. "The Quest for Excellence in University Teaching." *Journal of Higher Education,* 1987, *58,* 66–84.

Wotruba, T. A., and Wright, P. L. "How to Develop a Teacher-Rating Instrument: A Research Approach." *Journal of Higher Education,* 1975, *46,* 653–663.

John A. Centra is professor and chair of the Higher Education Program at Syracuse University.

Peggy Bonesteel is research assistant in the Higher Education Program at Syracuse University.

Student evaluations of instruction are often misunderstood or are met with direct hostility. Ratings "systems" are often very unsystematic indeed; at worst, they are seen as the punitive arm of administration. But ratings systems can provide vital information. How can their potential be realized?

Student Ratings in the Context of Complex Evaluation Systems

Michael Theall, Jennifer Franklin

Student "evaluations" are a corrupt practice of the '60s, one of the many from that era that I hope will be completely forgotten. They are an easy sop to the students from administrators . . . who are unwilling or unable to do anything to really improve teaching. . . . I happen to think that there are some really rotten teachers . . . who should be forced to shape up or leave. But that's a job for strong deans and chairmen, not student "evaluators" and educationists like yourself.
          —Anonymous quotation from faculty responses to a survey
             on student ratings, conducted by the authors

It seems that Kenneth Eble was right when he said (1983, p. 65), "No corner of the university . . . lacks faculty members who fulminate against student evaluations, with little or no examination of the large body of research . . . that underlies the practice." But what about this "large body of research"? What does it tell us? Marsh (1987, p. 255) succinctly summarizes student ratings as "1) multidimensional; 2) reliable and stable; 3) primarily a function of the instructor who teaches a course rather than the course that is taught; 4) relatively valid against a variety of indicators of effective teaching; 5) relatively unaffected by a variety of variables hypothesized as potential biases; and 6) seen to be useful by faculty . . . by students . . . and by administrators." Marsh's conclusions agree with those found in other major reviews of the past twenty years (Centra, 1989; Costin, Greenough, and Menges, 1971; McKeachie, 1979). Past student-ratings research has concentrated largely on methodological and measurement issues and on the dissemination of this literature—a reasonable focus, given that the student-ratings process is indeed a measurement event. Some writers have offered guidelines (at various levels of detail) for the development of evaluation programs that include ratings (Braskamp, Brandenburg, and Ory, 1984; Centra, 1979; Doyle, 1983; Aleamoni, 1987; Miller, 1987; Seldin, 1984).

Thus, student ratings are seen to fill needs felt by students, administrators, and many faculty. The increased use of and reliance on student ratings in colleges and universities across the country (Seldin, 1989) is testament to the practicality of using ratings as a simple means of collecting evaluation data. But if there is consensus among researchers, and increasingly widespread acceptance of the practice of collecting ratings, why are campus debates on the issue frequently so acrimonious? Why are users of student-ratings data so often unaware of even the most fundamental precepts of the literature (Franklin and Theall, 1989)? What is wrong with ratings practice? Are student ratings falling short of the goals they were intended to serve?

Miller (1987) offers four characteristics of evaluation systems, which help to explain this phenomenon. He notes that such systems often evolve haphazardly, are sources of dissatisfaction by virtue of their very purpose, can never be expected to achieve full acceptance or provide complete satisfaction, and are legally questionable. Despite their ubiquity, it seems that ratings have not (and perhaps could not have) become a fully effective part of the everyday processes of personnel decision making and teaching improvement.

The weaknesses of ratings systems have little to do with the validity and reliability of ratings themselves. Ineffective use of ratings can very easily come about when policy is unclear, when there is no faith in the reliability of data-collection procedures, or when reports of results are disseminated without regard for how they may be used or by whom. Merely having valid and reliable student data in no way ensures that the information will be used appropriately or effectively.

As academics, many ratings participants have some familiarity with at least one aspect of ratings (such as the methodologies for survey questionnaires or data processing), and yet they lack a more comprehensive view, failing to see ratings systems as one part of evaluation systems, which in turn are one part of instructional systems. Further, these systems are fit into departments, colleges, and institutions. At each level, new pressures are brought to bear, and new requirements are imposed, because the purposes, standards, users, and uses of the system change. For example, at the college or institutional level, consider the problem of comparing the performance of faculty from different disciplines. As Cashin notes in Chapter Eight, differences across disciplines can affect ratings results; departments and institutions must decide how to deal with these differences when personnel decisions are made. Can a teacher of English composition be compared fairly to someone teaching a course in physics, even with classes of the same size at the same level? The answer is maybe, but only *if* the comparison is on a general construct (such as overall teaching effectiveness) *and if* very careful and complete analysis of institutional norms shows ratings in the two departments to be similar (with no significant differences between means on the item for classes of similar size, level, and nature), *and if* such comparisons are allowable under institutional policy, *and especially if* those who make the decision are aware of all the factors just enumerated.

Student ratings "systems" are made up of more than questionnaires, machine-scorable answer sheets, and computer-generated reports of results. Regardless of the qualifications of their users, ratings systems are complex aggregations of functional components and processes that act together to collect, analyze, report, or help users employ students' perceptions of the instruction they have received. Such aggregations may be chaotic and poorly articulated, or they may be "default" systems churning out incoherent noise. Conversely, they may be systematically planned and implemented to provide valid, useful information. They are never simple, although they are often treated simplistically.

Any organized effort to collect ratings requires development and implementation of processes that involve faculty, students, administrators, and institutional resources. Ratings processes operate in the contexts of policy, politics, and philosophy. They may affect faculty satisfaction and motivation and, ultimately, such instructional outcomes as student achievement, satisfaction, and retention. Whether ratings processes ultimately work to provide valid, reliable information about teaching performance depends both on the quality of the processes used to obtain the information and on the ability of receivers to use it appropriately. Ratings systems are used to tell people who have a serious investment in their profession how well they are performing in at least one part of their job. Unfortunately, these systems often make this sensitive information public, without regard to the quality of the information or the qualifications of those who will use it. The scope of bad practice is unknown, but it seems more likely when ratings systems are developed without a synoptic, coherent overview and when practice is not governed by a clear process derived from the accepted literature.

The consensus of evaluation writers and researchers (Theall and Franklin, 1989) is that literature in the field must expand beyond measurement questions and begin to see student-ratings issues and problems as complex configurations of events that are faced on a day-to-day basis by faculty, administrators, and practitioners. As Manicas and Secord (1983, p. 399) note, "Events are the conjunctures of structured processes and are always the outcome of complex causal configurations at the same, and at many different, levels." For evaluation researchers, the task is to conduct new kinds of investigations into questions about "complex causal configurations," and it means bringing past and present research into everyday practice, in clear and useful ways. It appears that "qualitative" (Fetterman, 1988) or "naturalistic" (Lincoln and Guba, 1985) methods would be very useful in investigating and understanding these configurations.

An understanding of ratings systems requires knowledge of general theory and specific knowledge of the variables involved, as well as their effects on and relationships to one another. The development of coherent ratings systems requires systematic descriptions, organizational entities, resources, and links among them in real instructional environments. Handbooks on evaluation (Millman, 1981; Doyle, 1983; Braskamp, Brandenburg, and Ory, 1984) have made great strides in identifying issues for practitioners, but more work remains to be done on conceptualizing the realm of practice. The more we as researchers know about the complexities of ratings systems, the more we can develop the knowledge that we need (in our other role, as practitioners) to recognize, link, and use all the parts of the systems in our practice.

Our immediate goal is to facilitate this new direction for inquiry and action, by describing student ratings as systems in the context of larger systems and by regarding research and practice as necessarily concurrent and complementary activities. We view ratings in terms of the goals they serve, their functional components, and the conditions that influence or determine the outcomes they achieve. To that end, this chapter offers some schemata for classifying the components and processes of ratings systems, as well as the settings in which they operate. We are not doing this purely as an exercise in model building; it is crucial to good evaluation practice that we know and account for interactions and relationships within the system. The model we present here is intended to illustrate these multidimensional relationships economically and graphically.

Where does a systematic evaluation process begin? It starts with analysis of the context and conditions of the situation, the needs of the system's users, and the role that the evaluation will play. There are certainly precedents to this approach. Scriven (1967) has noted the importance of the role intended for any evaluation, particularly with respect to whether the evaluation is "formative" or "summative." The role determines, to some extent, whether the information collected will be concerned with "instrumental" (process) or "consequential" (outcome) data; in any case, however, evaluation's primary goal is always the same: an estimation of merit, worth, or value. Stake (1967) proposes a "judgment matrix" that incorporates "antecedents," "transactions," and "outcomes" in arriving at judgments based on specified "standards." Stufflebeam's (1968) "CIPP" model stresses context, input, process, and product as the categories of evaluative concern. Whether we choose "antecedents" or "context," the starting point is the situation(s) in which evaluation takes place.

In his discussion of the effects of context and environment on teacher evaluation in public schools, McKenna (1981) offers an ecological paradigm: What "ecologies" are of concern in this discussion? At the broadest level, the influence of the external context must be acknowledged. What are some of the influencing factors? A partial list might include local and national government, the general economy and the particular condition of the local economy, politics, current and potential funding, social attitudes, and other factors. For example, Apps (1988) describes how the needs and demands of society can shape (and be shaped by) higher education.

Another so-called ecological system encompasses the institution and its environment. In the case of multisite state systems, another layer of context is added. Geis (1984), in his discussion of the context of evaluation, refers to the way institutions have changed from "monastery to industry." The history, nature, direction, type, reputation, and location of an institution will affect its policies and, thus, its evaluation systems. The target clients of the institution (intended students, as well as the world they will enter after graduation) will influence policy and direction. With respect to evaluation policy and procedures, the words and actions of the institution's leaders will have a profound effect. If the message from leaders is that promotion and tenure are based on scholarship, then the nature, uses, and effects of evaluation will not be the same as at an institution that puts teaching first. This does not necessarily mean that evaluation and ratings systems will be better or more widely accepted at the teaching-oriented institution. In fact, when ratings form the basis of personnel decisions, the chances for opposition to ratings are perhaps even greater. The presence and status of faculty organizations or unions will also affect policy, particularly concerning the extent to which that policy is negotiable, public, and part of a formal contract. Birnbaum's (1988) discussion of the "cybernetics" of academic organizations offers very useful insights into how different kinds of institutions operate, and his four models of institutional types (collegial, bureaucratic, political, and organized anarchy) clearly differ in their approaches to and implementations of personnel decision-making procedures.

Within institutions, college and departmental differences represent the final level of environmental context and layers of complexity. The same categories of impact are at work here as at the institutional level. Consider, for example, the often heard comparison that says colleges of nursing emphasize teaching and interpersonal interaction with students, while colleges of engineering deliberately make their courses difficult and offer little help to students, on the theory that they have to weed out those students who "can't hack it." We have not encountered research that substantiates or refutes this proposition; such investigation would certainly shed light on the ways in which different departments view, treat, and use student-ratings data. We can, however, report an anecdote from first-hand experience.

A faculty member publicly proposed that student ratings should be weighted, so that "A" students' ratings would be worth four points, "B" students' ratings would be worth three points, and so on, with no value assigned to failing students' ratings. This person would be surprised to read Theall, Franklin, and Ludlow's (1990) report that "A" and "B" students provided 69.7 percent (from a sample of 2,381 courses, with 47,732 individual respondents) of the "worst" ratings given on an "overall instructor" item, while "D" and "F" students provided only 11 percent of such ratings. The distribution of grades for the entire sample was very similar to this subset; thus, no conclusion could be drawn that poor students attempt to punish their instructors or that good students always rate their teachers highly. It seems that the instructor's (or department's) perception of the student rater may have as much to do with ratings interpretation and use as does the student's perception of the instructor.

Consider, too, the political problems of small departments, where the intimacies of personnel decisions are shared by everyone. What about the large department that offers required service courses and uses temporary instructors to teach them? Should evaluation policy be exactly the same for these teachers as for permanent staff? One generally accepted rule for faculty evaluation (see Arreola and Aleamoni, Chapter Three) is that multiple sources of data and/or several administrations of a student-ratings instrument are necessary for fair and methodologically correct evaluation. Does this rule apply here? Does the department have a responsibility to its students to review temporary instructors each term and avoid rehiring those who are poorly rated? Can ratings be legitimately used for this purpose? Each situation requires something different. How can we decide what evaluation process will be most effective?

Evaluation of Instruction in Context: An Information Matrix

We can begin by locating ratings systems within faculty evaluation settings in higher education. To portray the breadth and interrelationships of evaluation's concerns, we have devised a matrix of information needs for evaluation, predicated on the purposes of the evaluation, the nature of the users of evaluation results, and the sources of evaluative information. Figure 1 displays this realm of evaluation activity in three dimensions. Note that ratings are only one source of information in the model. Doyle (1983) offers such matrices ("cubic schemata") to structure the focuses, sources, and ways of transmitting information, but this matrix is oriented more toward assisting in decisions about the nature and extent of the information collected and about the people to whom it is reported and how reporting is done. From this general model, we will scale our discussion down to student-ratings systems and their uses. First, however, we offer an explanation of the overall matrix.

Figure 1. Evaluation Information Matrix

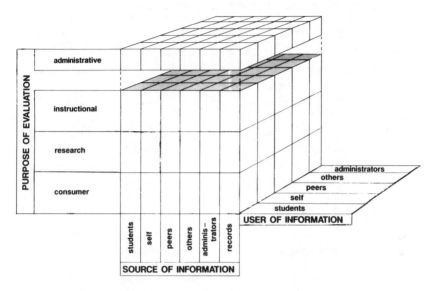

Purposes of Evaluation

At the left of the figure, some general purposes of evaluation are presented hierarchically with respect to the amount of information each purpose requires. Under the right conditions, data collected for a single purpose may be usable for multiple purposes. For example, some of the information collected for teaching improvement may also be used for decisions on promotion and tenure, as well as for inclusion in a catalogue of evaluation results for students' use in course selection. Even though the information is the same, however, the ways in which it is presented in these situations will be different (Theall, Franklin, and Birdsall, 1987). Another important issue is that when an effective system for evaluation is in place, it is inherently able to couple data-collection routines and analysis for teacher and course evaluation, on the one hand, with investigations for separate purposes, on the other. Later in this chapter, we will present examples of the productive joining of evaluation data with other data for research in several different areas.

Users of Information

On the right side of the figure are the users of evaluation results. Although students frequently provide evaluative information, it is important to remember that they are evaluators only when the purpose of evaluation is course selection. In fact, the real evaluator is effectively the person who makes a judgment that is based on the data at hand. Thus, when student ratings of instruction are used for decisions about promotion, tenure, and merit, promotion and tenure committees, department chairs, or deans make the judgments and are the real evaluators. Such decisions carry great responsibility, as well as the implication that those who make such decisions should be knowledgeable, valid, reliable judges. Recent research (Franklin and Theall, 1989) has shown that many who make personnel decisions, based at least partly on student ratings, are unfamiliar with the most accepted and important literature in the field. This finding underscores the need for extreme caution in collecting, analyzing, and reporting data that may be used for personnel decision making, and it reinforces the importance of college and department systems and policies that protect both the individual and the institution.

Sources of Information

At the base of the figure are depicted common sources of information used when courses, instructors, or instructional events and programs are evaluated. These categories are generally self-explanatory, with the exception of the boxes marked "others" and "records."

"Others" means any valid observers or reporters and can include teaching-improvement experts or evaluators, faculty from other disciplines, or persons naive to the subject matter. The point to remember is that the role of the evaluation will guide choices made in this area. In personnel evaluation, the observer clearly must have the expertise to judge competence or quality. A third party brought in to judge, for example, the completeness and currency of course content must be knowledgeable if his or her comments are to be included in the dossier. For formative purposes, a range of expertise on the part of observers may be more valuable because naive observers may encounter difficulties similar to those experienced by students, but comments from such observers do not really belong in a dossier for promotion and tenure. Shore and others (1986) give several examples of what to include in a dossier and suggest useful guidelines for assembling and presenting such materials for decisions about promotion and tenure.

"Records" is a category that includes a number of items: the registrar's list of course grades, data about course enrollments, general advising, direction of dissertations and theses, alumni reports, publications, citation counts, and service to the university, the profession, and the community. The important point in gathering these data is to be aware of the emphases of the institution and the weight assigned to each type of activity. Remember also that the "records" category includes the number, type, forum, and quality of papers, presentations, and publications, as well as successful grant applications, research projects, and professional activities. In many cases, this is a most important set of numbers.

Seldin (1989) reports on the factors that colleges consider in evaluating overall faculty performance, as well as on the sources of information that colleges use to evaluate teaching performance. Four of Seldin's findings are noteworthy. First, the department chair remains the predominant source of information in faculty evaluation. Second, systematic use of student ratings has risen significantly, so that ratings have become the second most frequent source of data for teaching evaluation (only a fraction of a point behind the departmental chairperson's input). Third, classroom visits by colleagues have gained significantly, despite the many problems associated with the nonstandardized procedures often used in such visits. Fourth, scholarship, publications, and professional activities have increased in importance, although their position relative to other factors has remained the same. The implications of Seldin's study concern the importance of using multiple sources of data and of understanding the relative weights assigned to these sources by the institution, the college, and the department.

Synergism: A Useful Concept

Synergism is the joint action of discrete agencies, action whose total effect is greater than the sum of the agencies' effects when the agencies are acting independently. Synergism is not unidirectional, however; the combined effects of evaluative agencies can produce negative and damaging results, as well as positive and productive ones. Scenarios for two evaluation systems are described here to demonstrate these differences.

A Negative Synergistic System

The Context. A large research-oriented university, where emphasis on teaching varies by college and department, seeks a means of obtaining ratings data. There are two underlying reasons: a strong demand from students for a campuswide system of evaluation and publication of results (the students are politically active and quite insistent), and a need to bring evaluation results efficiently from a campuswide system into personnel decision making (this need is articulated only to the extent that this use of evaluative data is said to be planned for some point in the future and must be inexpensive). There are also rumors of faculty unionization; strong feelings on the issue have already surfaced.

The institution has no organized resources (that is, no agency for evaluation or teaching improvement) and no professional staff who are experienced or trained in developing or operating evaluation systems. The student newspaper regularly prints stories about the need for an evaluation system and about how student leaders ("us") have struggled against a slow and recalcitrant administration ("them") and against certain faculty who oppose evaluation (another "them"). Faculty are divided in their opinions, but even those who support student ratings are concerned that faculty ("us") will be targets of certain students who have trivial or vengeful agendas ("them"). Worse, faculty are also concerned that the administration (another "them") will use results capriciously or only for punitive purposes. The administration ("us") feels that its intent is honorable, that some students ("them") are being too demanding, and that some faculty (another "them") are subverting attempts to create a reasonable system. Negative synergism is already at work because the energies of the participants are at least partly turned toward self-protection, rather than toward a unified approach to solving a problem.

In time-honored fashion, a committee of faculty, students, and administrators is formed to review the issues and develop a proposal. Other committees representing the three groups are also created informally, and certain individuals take it upon themselves to investigate the issue. More negative synergism crops up here because the newly formed agencies are invested with different levels of authority and are reporting to different audiences. All these committees take the same path: to devise a questionnaire. Now there is even more negative synergism because each committee's investment in its own form will create dissension. Nevertheless, different forms are proposed; debate over questions ensues, and a compromise is reached on a questionnaire. Despite the questionnaire's intuitive appeal (based on items that are not so different from those seen on the sample forms used by the various committees), not all sides are pleased. More potential negativity appears at this point because dissatisfaction will lead to resistance to and subversion of the survey process.

The questionnaire includes items on overall rating of instructor and course, desire to take other courses from the same instructor, workload and difficulty, the instructor's "friendliness," the instructor's speaking ability and organization, the instructor's skill in using the blackboard, the instructor's fluency in English, and the instructor's punctuality, as well as items on readings, assignments, and tests. There is the potential for still more negativity here because all the items are considered equally important, all will be used for each intended purpose, and some are either technically incorrect or inappropriate for one or more of their intended uses. The items may be important in their own right (as in the case of fluency in English and its importance to students), but they are not useful for other purposes. How will instructors who are native speakers of English be compared to one another, or to non-native speakers? From one point of view, this question may even be discriminatory.

It is agreed that student government will be responsible for conducting the evaluations, that the computing center will process the forms and produce reports (one for the instructor, one for the department chair, one compiled report for publication), and that a faculty committee will oversee the entire process. More negative synergism occurs here because three separate groups are involved in the process, and no one administrator is really responsible for the quality or control of the system.

The Result. There is much hostility and suspicion in this system, particularly since reports are being forwarded directly to the administration. The system is inaccurate. It is often late in producing its reports, and most of those involved dislike it. Fewer and fewer courses get evaluated, because the turnover in student government makes it impossible to standardize data-collection procedures or train students in data collection. Long-standing departmental processes (some of which may be superior to the new system) either duplicate the effort or are disrupted. Several errors in operations lead to data from some instructors' courses being identified incorrectly as data from the courses of other instructors. The catalogue of results contains mean scores of the items, with no norms or other statistics for interpretation. Results get misused or misinterpreted. Finally, a lawsuit results because a professor is denied tenure on the basis of published results. The university loses the suit. Within three years, the system is dead.

This system's problems could not be attributed to any one person or any one group. Much effort was expended by many people, whose intentions were positive and honorable, but there was no systematic planning. The complexity of the problem, the initial misdirection, and the interactions of the agencies at work led to a series of mistakes in planning and execution. The agencies involved did not focus their efforts, and the result was conflict. The institution became "a house divided," and the demise of the system was predictable.

A Positive Synergistic System

The Context. A similar institution, facing similar demands, takes a broad view and begins its efforts by assessing and clarifying the needs of all interested groups. A unified committee is formed, but its tasks are clearly defined as twofold: to use external experts and identify the important steps that must be taken in developing and implementing a system, and to propose a set of goals that the system can profitably serve. When these tasks are completed, consensus is sought about the importance, relevance, and achievability of the goals. Finally, when a few clearly important goals are established, discussion about the system itself begins (with external experts recommended again, to avoid common technical, methodological, practical, administrative, and other errors). (One of the most successful efforts of this kind was at Miami–Dade Community College, where planning and consensus took place over a three-year period; see Jenrette, 1989.)

The institution defines its first goals as supporting and improving teaching and responding to students' needs for a voice. To this end, the following list of system requirements was developed:

1. Provide summary data for students' use in course selection, in the form of a published catalogue of results
2. Provide detailed data for confidential teaching improvement and, to the extent possible, provide assistance in gathering, interpreting, and using these data for improving teaching
3. Provide data for personnel decision making, including reports and institutional, college, departmental, or other appropriate norms
4. Provide data for institutional use, in the form of compiled results for colleges or departments and for faculty or student groups.

In effect, then, this should be a multipurpose system able to meet these various needs efficiently. This goal requires a cooperative effort on the part of several university agencies. For example, the registrar provides accurate information on courses and instructors, so that response sheets can be preprinted in the correct numbers and with correct information. The computing center provides support for data management and processing. The campus mail system gets ready for two or three large-scale distributions of materials each term. Departmental secretaries are aware of the system's needs for accurate information on courses and instructors, and they assist the evaluation agency by providing information about changes, dropped courses, and so on. The synergism of these agencies allows more accurate and timely operations than would be possible if individual units performed all tasks independently.

One element crucial to the success of the system was the determination that, despite the need for a cooperative effort, one unit should ultimately be responsible for the system's operation. It would be staffed by highly qualified, experienced individuals. There would be ongoing involvement of faculty, students, and administrators in this unit, to make the best use of the system and determine its future uses, but any discussions about the system and its uses would be guided by the expertise of this unit's staff. In other words, the process would be governed by the same systematic rules for planning and design that governed the development of the system itself. Details of operations and decisions about the kinds and formats of reports would be based on standards of practice drawn from the literature and on the specific needs of the institution. Clear policies for uses of data would be determined before any data were collected. Safeguards would be included to protect faculty, students, and the institution from errors and from misuse or misinterpretation of data. Finally, the system would undergo a field test for at least one year. During this period, no personnel decisions would be based on system reports. At year's end, decisions about further use of the system would await full reports on its administrative operation and on the validity and reliability of instruments, the development of norms, and the reactions of the system's clients.

The Result. This system has a better chance of success. No system is perfect, but the design of this one is sensitive to users' needs and has built-in flexibility and contingency plans. For example, let us assume that nowhere on campus is there a fully current and correct file of faculty's addresses. This means that some materials will not reach some faculty. Is time built in to the schedule of evaluation events to accommodate last-minute requests for materials? Is there a quality-control mechanism that prevents duplicate questionnaires from being used? Is there a way to detect whether Professor X mistakenly used Professor Y's materials because they were delivered to the wrong room? Is there a way to improve the accuracy of addresses or enlist departments in quality control of distribution once materials reach departmental offices?

The prognosis for this system is that it will meet the direct needs of its users and serve the institution well. Are there additional benefits? The following discussion demonstrates that there are many potential uses and benefits of a well-articulated, multipurpose system.

Synergism Within the System

Given the contexts of evaluation and the interrelationships of variables, what actually happens in a ratings system, and how would this system for evaluation work to accomplish various tasks? Figures 2 and 3 outline the tasks of such a system, as well as its theoretical foundations.

In Figure 2, the activities of evaluation and improvement are shown as threefold: collection and analysis of evaluation data; interpretation or reporting of data by practitioners, including any resulting prescriptions for improvement; and actual provision of references, materials, consultation, and resources to clients.

Figure 2. Activities of Evaluation and Teaching Improvement

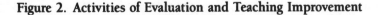

Data collection and analysis   References and resources

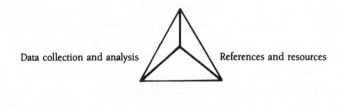

Interpretation   Prescription

Figure 3. Realms of Theory and Practice

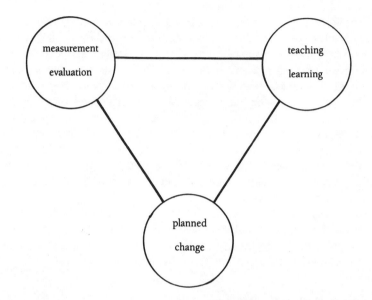

Figure 3 displays the realms of theory and practice that inform evaluation and improvement. *Measurement* and *evaluation* theory inform data collection and analysis. Theories of *planned change* (for example, those from communications, organizational development, and the diffusion and adoption of innovations) guide the ways in which data are interpreted and reported to clients. Theories of *teaching* and *learning* provide references and guide the development or use of resources.

Theory and practice do not operate independently, however. In a functioning system, there is constant interaction between the two. Figure 4 shows the interrelationships of research and theory with practice. The relationships between theory and practice are synergistic—that is, the activities of one area support and nourish those of the other. The multipurpose system for evaluation, improvement, and research depicted in Figure 4 not only offers direct evaluation and improvement services but also can develop knowledge about the realms of theory by using the data and experience gathered in practice. For example, evaluation can be used for research into student attitudes (Abbott and others, 1989), course improvement (Cronbach, 1963), curriculum design and review (Diamond, 1989), assessment (Gray, 1989), pedagogical research (Murray, 1985), research into teaching and learning (Stark and Mets, 1988; Theall, 1986), and psychological research (Yarbrough, 1989). These variables and the very nature of their interrelationships become targets for new directions in evaluation

Figure 4. A Multipurpose System for Evaluation, Improvement, and Research

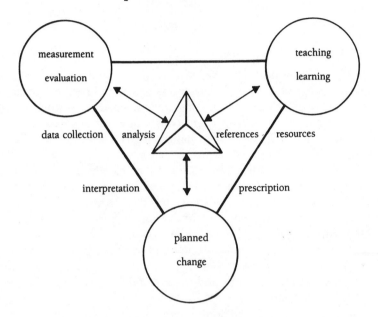

research. Just as the synergism of agencies within the institution can produce unexpected benefits, so can the synergism of research and practice produce valuable results when data collected and processed for one purpose complement data used for other purposes.

This system can help with institutional research (for example, analysis of evaluations and performance of beginning or "at risk" students). It can provide information for such teaching-improvement activities as the training of teaching assistants (Nyquist, Abbott, and Wulff, 1989), based on analysis of evaluations gathered from courses taught by teaching assistants in various subjects. The system can also involve faculty in research or development projects supported by internal or external funding (for example, such a system has been used at Northeastern University to identify faculty exceptionally skilled at using class time, who then helped to develop a teaching-improvement unit on this topic; see Theall, Sorcinelli, Sorcinelli, and Franklin, 1989).

The positive interactions of the agencies in our example create more benefits than the originally envisioned system was seen to contain. This is possible not only because the operations and services of the system are defined by the context and by the needs of the system's clients but also because the system is run as a coherent whole by persons with appropriate expertise and authority and with overall responsibility for operations. Institutional commitment and communication are the other essential elements of success.

Conclusion

Teaching is a multidimensional activity, and student ratings reflect the variety and range of teaching behaviors, as well as the successes or failures of those who practice its art, craft, and science. Nevertheless, while researchers, practitioners, and clients of ratings systems all acknowledge the multidimensionality of ratings, these parties have not brought the multifunctionality of ratings to bear on other issues of importance to faculty, students, and institutions. From inside an efficiently operating student-ratings system, we can conduct research and provide services to the users of evaluation, as well as to those who supply data for the system's purposes. An understanding of the contexts of evaluation is crucial, as is the concomitant ability to identify how the intended uses and audiences of evaluation affect the kinds of data collected and the ways in which results are reported. To use a ratings system without appropriate concern for the protection of faculty, students, and the institution is to misuse the system and defeat its purpose.

The consensus of evaluation writers and researchers is that the psychometrics of ratings are no longer the most important focus of research. In fact, it is the interrelationship—the synergy—of research and practice that deserves our attention. These new directions in evaluation are centered on better understanding of teaching itself, of the variables at work when teaching or evaluation take place, and of the ways in which evaluation results are presented and used. We no longer look only for variables that may bias evaluation; we also look for ways in which research and practice may inform each other, help us answer questions about teaching and learning, and lead to better-informed decisions about people, programs, and performance.

References

Abbott, R. D., Wulff, D. H., Nyquist, J. D., Ropp, V., and Hess, C. W. "Further Evidence Regarding Students' Satisfaction with Processes of Collecting Student Opinions About Instruction." Paper presented at the annual meeting of the American Educational Research Association, San Francisco, 1989.

Aleamoni, L. M. "Evaluating Instructional Effectiveness Can Be a Rewarding Experience." *Journal of Plant Disease*, 1987, 71, 322–329.

Apps, J. W. *Higher Education in a Learning Society: Meeting New Demands for Education and Training.* San Francisco: Jossey-Bass, 1988.

Birnbaum, R. *How Colleges Work: The Cybernetics of Academic Organization and Leadership.* San Francisco: Jossey-Bass, 1988.

Braskamp, L. A., Brandenburg, D. C., and Ory, J. C. *Evaluating Teaching Effectiveness: A Practical Guide.* Newbury Park, Calif.: Sage, 1984.

Centra, J. A. *Determining Faculty Effectiveness: Assessing Teaching, Research, and Service for Personnel Decisions and Improvement.* San Francisco: Jossey-Bass, 1979.

Centra, J. A. "Faculty Evaluation and Faculty Development in Higher Education." In J. C. Smart (ed.), *Higher Education Handbook of Theory and Research.* Vol. 5. New York: Agathon Press, 1989.

Costin, F., Greenough, W. T., and Menges, R. J. "Student Ratings of College Teaching: Reliability, Validity, and Usefulness." *Review of Educational Research,* 1971, *41,* 511-535.

Cronbach, L. J. "Course Improvement Through Evaluation." *Teachers College Record,* 1963, *64,* 672-683.

Diamond, R. M. *Designing and Improving Courses and Curricula in Higher Education: A Systematic Approach.* San Francisco: Jossey-Bass, 1989.

Doyle, K. O. *Evaluating Teaching.* Lexington, Mass.: Heath, 1983.

Eble, K. E. *The Aims of College Teaching.* San Francisco: Jossey-Bass, 1983.

Fetterman, D. M. *Qualitative Approaches to Evaluation in Education.* New York: Praeger, 1988.

Franklin, J., and Theall, M. "Who Reads Ratings: Knowledge, Attitudes, and Practices of Users of Student Ratings of Instruction." Paper presented at the annual meeting of the American Educational Research Association, San Francisco, 1989.

Geis, G. L. "The Context of Evaluation." In P. Seldin (ed.), *Changing Practices in Faculty Evaluation: A Critical Assessment and Recommendations for Improvement.* San Francisco: Jossey-Bass, 1984.

Gray, P. J. (ed.). *Achieving Assessment Goals Using Evaluation Techniques.* New Directions for Higher Education, no. 67. San Francisco: Jossey-Bass, 1989.

Jenrette, M. *The Teaching/Learning Project: Summary Report, 1988-1989.* Miami, Fla.: Miami-Dade Community College District, 1989.

Lincoln, Y. S., and Guba, E. G. *Naturalistic Inquiry.* Newbury Park, Calif.: Sage, 1985.

McKeachie, W. J. "Student Ratings of Faculty: A Reprise." *Academe,* Oct. 1979, 384-397.

McKenna, B. H. "Context/Environment Effects in Teacher Evaluation." In J. Millman (ed.), *Handbook of Teacher Evaluation.* Newbury Park, Calif.: Sage, 1981.

Manicas, P. T., and Secord, P. F. "Implications for Psychology of the New Philosophy of Science." *American Psychologist,* 1983, *38,* 399-413.

Marsh, H. W. "Students' Evaluations of University Teaching: Research Findings, Methodological Issues, and Directions for Future Research." *International Journal of Educational Research,* 1987, *11,* 253-388.

Miller, R. I. *Evaluating Faculty for Promotion and Tenure.* San Francisco: Jossey-Bass, 1987.

Millman, J. (ed.). *Handbook of Teacher Evaluation.* Newbury Park, Calif.: Sage, 1981.

Murray, H. G. "Classroom Teaching Behaviors Related to College Teaching Effectiveness." In J. G. Donald and A. M. Sullivan (eds.), *Using Research to Improve Teaching.* New Directions for Teaching and Learning, no. 23. San Francisco: Jossey-Bass, 1985.

Nyquist, J. D., Abbott, R. D., and Wulff, D. H. (eds.). *Teaching Assistant Training in the 1990s.* New Directions for Teaching and Learning, no. 39. San Francisco: Jossey-Bass, 1989.

Scriven, M. "The Methodology of Evaluation." In R. W. Tyler, R. M. Gagné, and M. Scriven (eds.), *Perspectives on Curriculum Evaluation.* Skokie, Ill.: Rand McNally, 1967.

Seldin, P. (ed.). *Changing Practices in Faculty Evaluation: A Critical Assessment and Recommendations for Improvement.* San Francisco: Jossey-Bass, 1984.

Seldin, P. "How Colleges Evaluate Professors." *AAHE Bulletin*, 1989, *41*, 3-7.

Shore, B. M., Foster, S. F., Knapper, C. K., Nadeau, G. G., Neill, N., and Sim, V. W. *The Teaching Dossier: A Guide to Its Preparation and Use*. (Rev. ed.) Montreal: Canadian Association of University Teachers, 1986.

Stake, R. E. "The Countenance of Educational Evaluation." *Teachers College Record*, 1967, *68*, 523-540.

Stark, J. S., and Mets, L. A. (eds.). *Improving Teaching and Learning Through Research*. New Directions for Institutional Research, no. 57. San Francisco: Jossey-Bass, 1988.

Stufflebeam, D. L. *Evaluation as Enlightenment for Decision Making*. Columbus: Evaluation Center, Ohio State University, 1968.

Theall, M. "Using Student Ratings of Instruction to Investigate Teaching and Learning." Paper presented at the first Research Forum on Postsecondary Teaching and Learning, Ann Arbor, Mich., 1986.

Theall, M., and Franklin, J. "Two Different Worlds: Research and Practice in Faculty Evaluation." *Instructional Evaluation*, 1989, *10*, 10-19.

Theall, M., Franklin, J., and Birdsall, M. "The Development of a Computer-Based, Diagnostic-Prescriptive System for Evaluation and Teaching Improvement." Paper presented at the second National Conference on Faculty Evaluation and Development, Orlando, Fla., 1987.

Theall, M., Franklin, J., and Ludlow, L. H. "Attributions and Retributions: Student Ratings and the Perceived Causes of Performance." Paper presented at the annual meeting of the American Educational Research Association, Boston, 1990.

Theall, M. (exec. producer), Sorcinelli, G. (producer, author), Sorcinelli, M. D. (producer, author), and Franklin, J. (instruct. designer). *Effective Use of Time in the College Classroom*. (Videotape and workbook.) Boston: Northeastern University Office of Instructional Development and Evaluation, 1989.

Yarbrough, D. B. "A Cognitive Psychological Perspective on Teacher Evaluation." *Journal of Personnel Evaluation in Education*, 1989, *2*, 215-228.

Michael Theall is associate professor and director of the Center for Teaching and Learning at the School of Education, University of Alabama, Birmingham.

Jennifer Franklin is senior research associate at the Center for Applied Social Research and manager of the Office of Instructional Evaluation at Northeastern University.

PART TWO

Perspectives on Practice

Decisions made in developing evaluation systems and the
small details of operation can render even the most sophisticated
measurement instruments useless. What are the important practical
considerations that can help institutions avoid these problems?

Practical Decisions in Developing and Operating a Faculty Evaluation System

Raoul A. Arreola, Lawrence M. Aleamoni

The literature in the field of faculty evaluation contains an abundance of research concerning the theoretical and psychometric underpinnings of a variety of forms, questionnaires, and procedures used in the evaluation of faculty performance. Less attention has been paid to the fundamental, practical, everyday issues and problems that face those responsible for actually operating fully functioning faculty evaluation programs. Based on the experience of designing, developing, and operating several large-scale faculty evaluation systems in a university setting, this chapter addresses some of those practical issues.

Purpose of the System

From a practical standpoint, it should be recognized that any faculty evaluation system must ultimately serve both a formative and a summative purpose. Faculty evaluation systems that start out ostensibly as formative (designed to provide feedback for the purpose of facilitating professional growth and development) almost always end up serving a summative purpose as well. Sooner or later, a faculty member will submit evaluation data as part of the evidence in support of a decision on promotion, tenure, or merit pay. Conversely, an administrator will ask for certain evaluative data to assist in making a difficult decision concerning a faculty member.

In practice, a single faculty evaluation system can be made to serve both formative and summative purposes. The key in developing and operating such a system is to carefully determine and prescribe the types of data to be gathered and what is to be done with them. The faculty evaluation system should be constructed in such a way that detailed, frequently gathered data are provided, in confidence, only to the faculty member concerned, for diagnostic and feedback purposes. Specified formats for summarizing the detailed data should be developed, but in no case should any particular term's detailed evaluative information concerning a faculty member be used for administrative decision making. The detailed data should provide the basis of self-improvement or faculty development only. The principle to be followed in preparing summary data for administrative purposes is to make certain that the summary data convey a sense of a faculty member's overall performance across time, and not just a single term's performance, whether that performance was good or bad.

Data Storage and Confidentiality

It is assumed that virtually any faculty evaluation system will gather information from students, peers, and administrators, as well as from various other sources, according to the specific design of the system. From a practical standpoint, a way must be developed for maintaining confidentiality while the data are being stored. There are basically two approaches: the centralized departmental file, and the individualized portfolio.

Centralized Departmental Files. A number of institutions place responsibility for gathering and storing faculty evaluation data with the departmental or divisional chair. In this system, a centralized file location is specified, and the chair (or the departmental secretary) controls access to the files. This approach places responsibility for security and confidentiality with two people—namely, the departmental chair and the departmental secretary. The advantage of this approach is that it is relatively unlikely that anyone will systematically violate the integrity of the information stored. There are a number of disadvantages, however. First and foremost, this system creates a great deal of work for the departmental chair if the department is relatively large. Second, if faculty perceive the central files as the primary evidence on which the administration will base decisions, there is a pronounced tendency for faculty to put voluminous amounts of material in their files—just to be safe. As work expands to fill the time allotted to it, evaluation files tend to grow in proportion to the space available. Finally, faculty may feel that the confidentiality of the information has already been compromised, since the chair, as an "administrator," will have already seen it. If the departmental chair is serving as the chief faculty development officer, however, as is sometimes the case, this approach can be very effective, especially in relatively small departments.

The Portfolio System. A system that appears to be gaining in popularity is the so-called portfolio system. With such a system, faculty members themselves are responsible for assembling and maintaining their files, in a specified style and format, to create their own evaluation portfolios. The portfolio generally contains clear, step-by-step instructions concerning the gathering of the evaluation data (such as published articles, syllabi, and examples of tests). Various summary and data-recording sheets are provided, so that faculty members can assemble, in a consistent and standardized fashion, the aggregate statistical data that are to be used for personnel decisions.

The advantage of this approach is that each faculty member is responsible for assembling his or her own evaluation data. No one person is responsible for assembling the data for all faculty, as is the case in the centralized filing system. This approach assumes a high level of trust between faculty and administrators, since personnel decisions may rely heavily on the summary or aggregate data assembled in the portfolio.

Peer Review and Evaluation

In many faculty evaluation systems, peer review or peer evaluation plays an important political, if not psychometric, role. Although the idea of peer review is appealing to many faculty, peer review systems are touchy and complicated, at the very least. In practice, peer review components of faculty evaluation systems are one of the biggest sources of problems and confusion.

Generally, peer review involves a committee, sometimes made up of all tenured faculty or all senior faculty or some similar combination. The function of such a committee is to review all the evidence (student-ratings printouts, letters of recommendation, other peers' or colleagues' comments, articles published) and make a decision or a recommendation to administrators. When a number of faculty are submitting their materials for review at the same time, the task before the committee can become massive. In addition, such a committee often brings subjective impressions, friendships, and hostilities into the decision-making process. This approach also has the unfortunate side effect of giving second-hand information or hearsay evidence much greater impact than it should have. Committee members may offer positive or negative opinions concerning the faculty member's teaching performance, and these may be based on random or limited comments from students.

Peer Review: The Best-Source Model. In practice, peer review should limit itself to using colleagues or peers to provide information that requires a professional perspective, or for which peers are the primary and best source of information. If peer input is to be gathered about a faculty member's classroom performance, then the faculty evaluation system should specify a visitation policy or procedure. Guidelines must be developed that clearly specify what behavior or performance is to be observed and rated.

Ideally, a training program should be set up to prepare faculty peers to be accurate and reliable observers.

Practical experience leads to the suggestion that this peer review model be restricted to areas of professional performance that require knowledge of the content field of the faculty member (for example, assessing the correctness and completeness of the content of a given course, or judging the contribution that a given article makes to the literature in the faculty member's field). In any case, the recommended procedure for peer evaluation is to gather only that information from faculty peers for which they are the primary and best source. Evaluation systems that ask a peer committee to review the ratings of students, or other such evaluative information, and then to produce another, single evaluation, based on their deliberations, tend to create more problems than they solve.

Peer Review: The Triad Model. If separate peer review committees are required to make such summary judgments, a good form to follow is the three-member, or triad, peer committee structure. Here, a three-person peer committee is appointed for every faculty member. One member is selected by the departmental chair, one is selected from a group of peers recommended by the faculty member being evaluated, and one is appointed from the faculty at large. In this way, no one faculty member has to sit on more than three peer review committees, and each committee concerns itself with only one faculty member.

With this approach, the member appointed from the faculty at large does not necessarily have to be from the same field as the person being evaluated. The primary function of the at-large member is to ensure that proper deliberative processes, prescribed by the evaluation system, are followed. It is assumed that the other two members will adequately represent the perspective of professionals from the content field. Moreover, since the faculty member being evaluated will have nominated one person on the committee, it is unlikely that negative biases on the part of the other two members will unduly affect the outcome of the committee's deliberations. Likewise, any unwarranted positive biases on the part of the two content-field peers will be offset by the assumed neutrality of the at-large member.

Since the triad committee concerns itself with only one faculty member, it is much easier to assign it more detailed and evaluatively relevant tasks. Such tasks may include in-depth assessment of course design, course materials, examinations, published articles, professional development, or any of a host of activities and roles that peers are best qualified to judge.

Practical Considerations in Operating a Student-Ratings System

Easily the largest and most visible component of a faculty evaluation system is the student-ratings form and its computerized output. Over the years, for good or for ill, student ratings have come to be the single most important component of faculty evaluation systems. Unfortunately, this has led to a plethora of student-ratings instruments developed by faculty, students, administrators, and committees. We do not necessarily endorse this situation, but from a practical perspective we must acknowledge it and deal with the problems that arise from designing and operating a large-scale student-ratings system.

Designing the System Environment. In keeping with the concept of designing and operating the faculty evaluation system to serve formative as well as summative purposes, several issues related to student-ratings systems must be stated before guidelines are proposed. It must be recognized that the value of any student-ratings system relies on students' confidence that their input will cause them no harm and have some effect on the instructor (Arreola, 1987). In practice, the operation of a student-ratings system requires careful balancing of the needs and concerns of students, faculty, and administrators. These needs and concerns are sometimes antithetical. This fact often places the person in charge of the student-ratings system in a very difficult position. On the one hand, faculty may be fearful and distrustful of the administration, going through a predictable set of stages in resisting or attempting to escape from an evaluation system (Arreola, 1983). On the other hand, students are fearful of retributions from faculty if they give negative ratings, or they may not believe that faculty or administrators will pay any attention to what they say. Finally, administrators may desperately want any kind of quantitative or "hard" data on which to base difficult personnel decisions.

Guidelines. Long experience with these circumstances leads to the following practical guidelines for running a student-ratings system:

1. If at all possible, never locate a student-ratings coordination or processing agency in the office of a dean, vice-president, or other major administrator. Such placement only reinforces the idea that the student-ratings system and the faculty evaluation office are simply "watchdog" agencies of the administration.

2. Try to locate the student-ratings form processing office in a test-scoring center, the computing center, the media center, or, ideally, in a faculty development center.

3. Arrange the processing schedule so that completed analyses of the student-ratings forms are not available until after final grades have been reported.

4. Conduct a program to maintain students' faith in the student-ratings system. Establish regular contact with student government. Appoint student representatives to the faculty evaluation and development committee. Include stories about the use of student ratings in the student newspaper at least once each term. Constantly inform students that faculty members will not see student ratings results until after grades have been

reported, and that student ratings are taken seriously by the faculty and the administration (Arreola, 1983). Without such a campaign, the student-ratings system will develop serious problems, including refusal of students to complete forms appropriately and seriously, if at all.

5. Make it clear that the processing office is a service to the faculty, not to the administration or student government. Do not automatically send results of the ratings to the administration or the student newspaper unless written permission has been given by instructors. Such actions will forever taint the credibility of the processing office. Require anyone who wants information about student ratings to get them from the faculty member concerned.

6. Make certain that distribution of copies of faculty evaluation print-outs is a matter between administrators and faculty or between students and faculty. Provide faculty members with multiple copies of analyses or other results; do not keep copies in the processing office. Make it physically difficult to recover or reconstitute a given faculty member's analysis. The best approach is to maintain only raw data files on tape. Then, if a request is received by the processing office to provide copies of a particular faculty member's evaluation results, it can truthfully be said that the processing office has no copies, but that the faculty member has several. The confidentiality and distribution of evaluation results should be a matter between faculty members and the administration, not between the processing office and the administration. The processing office must not be perceived as an arm of an intrusive administration.

Designing a Student-Ratings Form

Student-ratings instruments are frequently developed by faculty, students, administrators, or committees who lack expertise in questionnaire design and scaling. Such instruments typically are not subjected to studies of their reliability and validity. Therefore, their results are easily influenced by such extraneous classroom variables as time of day, class size, and instructor's personality. For student ratings to be considered an integral part of a comprehensive instructional evaluation system, they must be both reliable and valid. As a practical matter, six steps must be followed in designing and selecting a student-ratings instrument.

Purpose of the Form. The first step is to determine the purpose of the instrument. One primary purpose is to provide formative evaluation information for faculty members to use in improving their instruction. Another is to provide summative evaluation information to colleagues, administrators, and students for use in decisions about promotion, tenure, merit, and course selection. A third purpose is to provide both formative and summative evaluation information.

Evaluative Elements. The second step is to specify the elements that will be addressed by the instrument. If the course is to be judged, there must be questions or statements addressing organization, structure, objectives, difficulty, pace, relevance, content, and usefulness. If instruction is to be judged, there must be questions or statements addressing method of presentation, student interaction, pacing, and level of difficulty. If the instructor is to be judged, there must be questions or statements addressing personal characteristics, skill, rapport, preparation, interest, and apparent commitment. If learning is to be judged, there must be questions or statements addressing the level of students' satisfaction, their perceived competence, and their desire to continue study in the field.

Types of Items. The third step in constructing a student-ratings form is to determine the types of items the instrument should contain. The accuracy of students' responses and the meaningfulness of the ratings to the instructor depend on the appropriateness of the items and response formats.

Low-Inference and High-Inference Items. If the purpose of gathering student ratings is to produce measures that require considerable inference from what is seen or heard in the classroom, then high-inference measures are needed. These measures are obtained as ratings of the instructor on such scales as "partial–fair," "autocratic–democratic," and "dull–stimulating." These measures are appropriate for summative (final and global) decisions about the instructor or the instruction. If the purpose is to produce measures that require the student to classify teaching behaviors according to relatively objective categories, then low-inference measures are needed. These measures are obtained as frequency ratings of the instructor on such scales as "gesturing," "variation in voice," "asking questions," and "praise and encouragement." These measures are appropriate for formative decisions about the instructor and instruction because it is easier to translate them into specific behaviors that can be used in instructional improvement.

Open-Ended and Closed-Ended Items. The use of open-ended (free-response) items usually produces a colorful array of responses in students' own words but provides very little representative (consensus) information for instructors to use in formative evaluation. Instructors like such responses, however, because they enjoy reading comments to which they can attach their own interpretations. The use of closed-ended (limited-response) items can provide accurate counts of the types of responses to each item. The most acceptable and common approach is to include both closed-ended and open-ended responses.

The type of closed-ended response one should ask for is largely determined by the type of question or statement being asked or made. When care is not taken to match appropriate responses to each question or statement, incongruous and unreliable responses will result. For example, an item stated as "Was the instructor's grading fair?" dictates a response of yes or no. If it is stated as "The instructor's grading was fair," a response along an "agree strongly" to "disagree strongly" continuum is dictated. Neutral or "don't know" responses should be used only when they represent necessary options; otherwise, they will be used by students who have opinions but are reluctant to offer them.

If a continuum format is used with only the end points anchored (Excellent 1 2 3 4 5 6 Horrible), it tends to produce unreliable responses. It is necessary for each response point along the continuum to be identified. Furthermore, the numbers must be replaced with acronyms or abbreviations, so that students will know what they are responding to. In general, the "agree strongly" to "disagree strongly" continuum is appropriate whenever an item is stated either positively or negatively. Another type of closed-ended response scale that can be used is one that requires elaborate behavioral descriptions along the continuum. These are called *behaviorally anchored rating scales* (Aleamoni, 1981).

Developing or Selecting Items. The fourth step is to develop or select the items. If one is developing the items, then it is important to prepare appropriate types and to have the items independently edited and reviewed by colleagues. If one is selecting items or instruments in their entirety, then a careful content analysis of the instruments and the items must be conducted.

Organizing Items. The fifth step is the organization of the items in the instrument. One has to decide how they are to be grouped and labeled, how they should be organized for easy reading and answering, and how and where responses should be recorded. If there is a logical or chronological flow to the items, then their organization on the form should reflect it. If there are only a few negative items, then one or two should appear very early in the instrument, to avoid positive-response-set mistakes. It is advisable to have negatively stated items in the instrument, but only if they can be stated negatively in a logical manner. Most questionnaire items can be grouped into subscales. If the original grouping is done on a logical basis, then an empirical analysis, using a statistical technique such as factor analysis, should be used to ensure that the grouped items represent a common scale.

Reliability and Validity. The sixth step, once an instrument has been constructed, is to determine its reliability and validity through experimental administration. Reliability may be defined in two ways: the first describes the instrument's ability to produce stable responses from one time to another in a given course; the second describes the consistency (or degree of agreement) among respondents. Since most student-ratings instruments ask students to respond to different aspects of the instructional setting (instructor, instruction, textbook, homework), reliability of the items and the subscales should be the major concern. If one cannot demonstrate that the items and subscales of a particular instrument can yield stable responses, then the data and resulting evaluations may be meaningless.

If the instrument contains highly reliable items and subscales, one needs to determine how consistent students' responses are. Once the reliability problem has been solved, attention should focus on the validity of student ratings. Logical validation is concerned with the question "What does the instrument measure?" Empirical validation is concerned with the question "To what extent does the instrument measure what it is intended to measure?" A logical validation requires judgment about the content-validity of the instrument. This is usually accomplished through careful construction of the instrument, so that it contains items and subscales that will yield measures in the areas considered appropriate by an individual or group of experts in the field under consideration. Empirical validation requires the use of criterion measures, against which student ratings may be compared. Validity studies normally report the magnitude of the correlation between criterion measures and student ratings. Here, the higher the correlation, the better the validity.

Types of Student-Ratings Systems

Keeping in mind the steps for designing or selecting a student-ratings instrument, as well as the need to conduct reliability and validity studies on the resulting instrument, let us now consider several different student-ratings systems that can be used.

Instructor-Constructed Systems. The least defensible type of system is one created by a particular instructor for a particular course. This really does not constitute a ratings system at all. It is generally the result of an attempt to do something about the pressure to have a student-ratings system, without really doing anything.

Instructor-Selected Systems. A more defensible type of system is one in which the instructor selects items from a finite pool and includes these with a standard section containing a few general items. One of the earliest examples of such a pool was the Purdue Cafeteria System, which provided a two-hundred-item catalogue. Instructors selected their items, which were then printed on an optically scanned answer sheet, along with five standard, general items. Normative data were provided only for the five general items. Derry (1977) reports that the average reliability of a Cafeteria rating form is .88. Other examples of this type are the Instructor and Course Evaluation System (ICES) of the University of Illinois, Urbana–Champaign; the Instructor Designed Questionnaire (IDQ) of the University of Michigan; and the Student Perceptions of Teaching (SPOT) of the University of Iowa (Abrami and Murphy, 1980).

Standard Form, Optional Items. The most defensible type of student-ratings system is one that has a standard section of items applicable to almost all courses and instructors, with optional sections that allow the instructor to select supplementary (or more diagnostic) items from a catalogue. One of the earliest and continuing examples is the Course/Instructor Evaluation Questionnaire (CIEQ) system, which provides a standard section of twenty-one items, on which normative data are provided by item; five subscales; and two optional twenty-one-item response sections that allow instructors to select up to forty-two additional items from a catalogue. Aleamoni and Stevens (1986) report test-retest reliabilities of from .81 to .94 for the twenty-one standard items, and from .92 to .98 for the subscales. Other examples of this type are the Instructional Development and Effectiveness Assessment system (IDEA) of Kansas State University, the Student Instructional Report (SIR) of Educational Testing Service, and the Student Instructional Rating (SIR) system of Michigan State University (Abrami and Murphy, 1980).

Multiple Standard Forms. Another type of system is one that consists of multiple standard forms. The instructor's only choice here concerns the type of form, not the items. The University of Washington's Instructional Assessment System (IAS) provides six forms to faculty: for small lecture-discussion courses, for large lecture courses, for seminars, for problem-solving courses, for skills-oriented or practicum courses, and for quiz sections. Reported reliabilities range from .15 to .34 for single raters and to .88 and above for classes of forty students (Abrami and Murphy, 1980).

Administration of Student-Ratings Systems

After an appropriate instrument has been developed or selected, administrative procedures need to be established. If possible, responsibility for managing and directing a campuswide program of administering student ratings should be placed with instructional development, evaluation, or testing personnel. One should avoid placing such responsibility with students or with faculty in individual departments or colleges, because the system's application would be restricted, and the possibility of a lasting program would be reduced. As a last option, responsibility may be assumed by the chief academic officer of the institution, but the danger of having the system perceived as a "watchdog" program increases.

The method of administering the instrument and gathering students' responses can determine the quality of the resulting data. It is advisable to administer the instrument formally in the classroom by providing standardized instructions and enough time to complete all items. If the instrument is administered informally, without standardized instructions or a designated time to fill it out, students tend not to take it seriously and may not bother to turn it in. Furthermore, if students are permitted to take the instrument home, very few instruments will be returned.

Managing Large-Scale Student-Ratings Systems. The following procedures have been used successfully in managing large-scale student-ratings systems. These procedures assume that faculty members are not the primary persons administering the rating forms in class to students:

1. Set up a log for maintaining control of form distribution and collection. This log should contain the name of the faculty member, the number of the course, and the size of enrollment. Such information is generally available from the registrar's office.

2. Prepare packets with at least five more forms than the official number of students in the course. Log in the actual number of forms sent to the instructor.

3. In addition to ratings forms, the packet should contain a standardized script, to be read when the forms are passed out, and a proctor-identification form. Upon receipt of the packet, the faculty member should remove the proctor-identification form and write the name of the student in the class who has been selected to administer the forms. The faculty member must sign the proctor-identification form and return it separately to the processing office. The processing office should log in the date of receipt of the form and the name of the student proctor.

4. After returning the proctor-identification form, the faculty member should give the packet to the student proctor. The proctor distributes the forms and reads a standardized script for administering the student-ratings form. In addition to information concerning the kind of pencil to use, the script says that the faculty member is not in the room, that the results of the ratings will not be returned to the instructor until after final grades have been turned in, and that students' responses will be an important part of the information considered in improving the course or making decisions about promotion, tenure, retention, and merit pay.

5. The proctor certifies that the student-ratings forms were administered in accordance with instructions, that the script was read as part of administration, and that the faculty member was not in the room.

6. Cross-checking items should be included that ask several questions: "Was the instructor in the room when this form was administered?" "Did the proctor read the administration directions out loud to the class?" "Do you have confidence that your responses will make a difference?"

7. After the forms are completed and returned to the proctor, they should all be placed in the envelope along with the proctor's certification and returned by campus mail to the processing office.

8. Upon receipt of the packet, the date should be logged in, and the name on the proctor's certification should be checked against the name reported by the instructor on the proctor-identification form. A count is made of incoming completed forms, to make sure that the number does not exceed the official enrollment figure for the class. The latter step is designed to discourage "stuffing" of completed student-ratings packets by students or, in some cases, by faculty themselves.

9. Before being machine-processed, the student-ratings forms must be visually scanned for stray marks. Students often doodle in the margins or simply cross out incorrect responses rather than erasing. These types of marks must be erased before the sheets can be processed. Experience has

shown that the processing office is well advised to buy electric erasers. The time and staff needs for carrying out this step are often much greater than can be anticipated, especially if the system is new and students are not yet familiar with the forms.

10. Log the date when the computer analysis and student-ratings forms were returned to the faculty member.

Options for Administration in Class. The foregoing ten steps assume that a student proctor, selected from the class itself, administers the rating form. Other options, some less desirable than others, are also possible.

Self-Administration. In systems where the instructor administers the questionnaire, he or she should also read the standard instructions after the forms have been distributed and then remain in the front of the room until all forms have been completed. The instructor may then select a student from the class to gather the completed forms and deposit them in the campus mail. As before, a statement should specify that the instructor will not see the results until after final grades have been turned in. The exception to this procedure is when the instructor has informed students that their responses will be used in a formative way, to improve the current course.

Administration by Student Government. Another option is to have representatives of student government administer the form, if faculty and administrators are willing for them to do it. The students administering the instruments should also read standard instructions and request that instructors leave. The student organization can use the campus newspaper to announce when the instruments are going to be used and how they will be administered, as a final cross-checking procedure.

Administration by Staff. If an administrator designates a staff member, the same procedures should be followed. This option should be avoided, however, unless there is no other way to ensure common administration of the instruments. Faculty and students tend to feel threatened if they know that an administrator is controlling and directing the process.

When the rating instrument is administered, students should have all necessary materials and should generally fill out the forms in their regular classrooms, near the beginning of the particular class session. Above all, students must be left with the impression that their frank and honest comments are desired, and not that this is their chance to get back at the instructor. If students get the impression that the instructor is not really interested in their responses, they will not respond seriously. If students fear that the instructor is going to see their responses before final grades are in, they will respond more positively and write very few comments, especially if they are asked to identify themselves. If the instrument is administered immediately before or after a major examination, students tend to respond inconsistently. If students are allowed to discuss the course and the instructor while filling out the forms, biases enter into their ratings.

Reporting Results

One of the most important aspects of any program is the method of reporting results. If results are not reported in an appropriate, accurate, and timely manner, the usefulness of the instrument and of the system as a whole will be seriously compromised. In tabulating and summarizing responses, the following procedures should be considered:

1. Item responses should be weighted (that is, given numerical values), in order to calculate descriptive statistics, and the descriptive statistics should be reported.
2. Results should be reported by item and subscale, as appropriate.
3. Results should be summarized by class section, department, college, and so on.

Directionality of Numerical Scale. When items are presented with defined response scales (such as "agree strongly," and so on), they should be weighted to reflect direction and ideal response when the results are tabulated and summarized. For example, if the response scale were weighted 4 ("agree strongly"), 3, 2, 1, it would indicate that the item was positively stated, with the ideal response being "agree strongly." With such a weighting, it is possible to calculate a mean and standard deviation for each item for a given class of students. The mean value indicates the average rating, and the standard deviation indicates how similar or dissimilar responses were. Thus, results can be reported for items as well as for subscales. The results can also be summarized and reported by class section and course or by selected courses, courses within a department, courses within a college, and courses within the university. Such complete reporting schemes permit meaningful comparisons, when necessary.

Distributing Results: Voluntary Systems. An important question in any system of reporting results is who will or should actually see them. If administration of the instruments is completely voluntary, then only faculty members should receive the results. As noted earlier, the processing office is ill advised to enter into an arrangement that places it between the faculty and the administration.

Distributing Results: Mandatory Systems. If administration of the form is mandatory, as in many systems, then every effort should be made to remove the processing office from the responsibility of distributing results directly. If the processing office has no choice, and if the system must be designed to provide faculty with the *option* of releasing copies of their results to other parties, then great effort must be taken to ensure that instructors feel no pressure to release results. In such circumstances, a procedure must be implemented that requires a written release from the instructor. The processing office would be well advised to consult with the college or university attorney in developing the wording of such a release. Every effort must be made to make faculty members aware of who will receive copies of their results, and how frequently. In no case should students' written comments be reported to administrators or student organizations, since those comments tend to be susceptible to widely discrepant, subjective interpretations.

Publishing Results. If the faculty or administration has entered into an agreement with the campus student organization to publish results of student ratings, every effort should be made to ensure fair and accurate reporting. Results are usually reported in a book divided by disciplines or content areas. Student-published books are usually promoted as guides for prospective students, as well as vehicles to encourage instructional improvement. Unfortunately, given the overzealousness of some student editors and the vendettas of others, such publications have tended merely to generate antagonistic relationships between rated faculty and student editors.

One vehicle that can be used to disseminate ratings to a wider segment of the student body is the student newspaper. The most effective way to present results is to do it in a positive manner; for example, only the highest-rated faculty and courses are reported. Whoever is responsible for publishing results for mass consumption should remember that accentuating the positive, rather than focusing on the negative, means better acceptance, continued participation, and potential improvement on the part of participating faculty. Attempts to be cute or to attack instructors usually result in short-lived systems, with serious negative repercussions.

Format of the Computerized Analysis

It has been assumed that virtually every operational student-ratings system produces some form of computerized analysis. This output may range from a simple frequency count (for each response to each item) to a very sophisticated printout showing normative data of various sorts. Experience has shown that most faculty react unenthusiastically to sophisticated printouts that contain page after page of indices, norms, graphs, and tables. Although professional standards demand that the analysis of student-ratings data be accurate and statistically sound, most faculty are not well versed in the intricacies of item analysis, measurement theory, or statistical analysis. Moreover, most have no real desire to become knowledgeable in these areas. Therefore, in order for the computerized analysis of results to provide useful information that can be acted on for self-improvement, an effort must be made to make these analyses user-friendly. One way of doing this is to provide a verbal summary sheet, which translates the statistical information into general statements.

If the rating form has five response choices per item, it is clear that a standard deviation approaching 2.00 would indicate a wide disparity of responses to the item. In such a case, the mean value of the item would have little meaning, other than to represent the numerical average of the responses. The computer program can be written to produce a statement such as the following: "On item 6, the standard deviation was 1.8. This can be interpreted to mean that there was *considerable disagreement* among the students on this item, and thus the average response should not be interpreted as representing a consensus rating by the class." The program can also present a statement such as this one: "On item 18, the average response was 2.1, and the standard deviation was .4. This can be interpreted to mean that the students rated you as being *moderately high* on this item, and there was a *high* degree of consensus among the students in this rating.

Ideally, such statements should be printed as either the first or the last page in a computer analysis, to be found easily. Obviously, the program must be written to make the proper interpretations of various combinations of data relative to the appropriate norms. The point is that, even though the processing office may produce reports that are statistically sophisticated and correct, it must never be forgotten that analyses, to be useful, must be understood and used by faculty. Again, as a practical guideline, providing computerized, written interpretations of statistical information listed in the printout has been found to be highly effective.

Interpreting and Using Results

Although we want our analyses to be user-friendly, they must still present data of sufficient clarity and detail to permit sophisticated interpretations. How accurately and meaningfully the results of student ratings are interpreted and used depends on the type of information provided to participating faculty members and other interested parties. The research on student ratings has revealed a definite positive-response bias, which needs to be addressed in interpreting and using results. If students are asked to respond to items on a 4-point scale, responses for positively stated items tend to be distributed as shown in Figure 1. The use of comparative (normative) data in reporting results can counteract the positive-response bias and result in a more accurate and meaningful interpretation of ratings. For example, comparative data gathered on freshman-level courses in a department allow instructors to determine how they and their courses are perceived in relation to the rest of the courses in the department. When such comparative data are not available, instructors will be interpreting and using results in a void, with very little substantiation for their conclusions and actions.

Once established on a representative number of courses, the normative data base should not change appreciably from year to year. Additional courses can be added to the normative data base without significant change

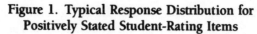

**Figure 1. Typical Response Distribution for
Positively Stated Student-Rating Items**

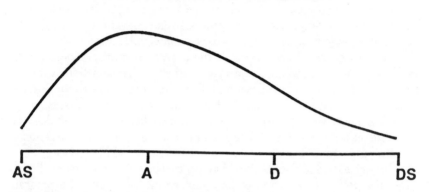

AS   **A**   **D**   **DS**

Note: AS = Agree Strongly; A = Agree; D = Disagree; DS = Disagree Strongly.

in distribution and comparative judgments. For some sources of invalidity identified as nontrivial by research studies (such as class level and required or elective status), comparative data stratified by course level and by required or elective status will provide meaningful interpretation of results. Aleamoni and Stevens (1986) include particular examples.

Qualitative judgments can also be provided to instructors through identification of mean intervals in the comparative data. These can be defined as representing levels of excellence or needed improvement. For example, the comparative data for freshman-level courses in a department can be divided into ten equal portions. Each portion can be defined as representing a 10 percent interval of rated courses, with a defined minimum and maximum course mean. These ten intervals can then be defined as follows: (1) Any course mean falling in the lowest 10 percent, 20 percent, or 30 percent interval is defined as poor and indicates that improvement is definitely necessary. (2) Any course mean falling in the 40 percent, 50 percent, 60 percent, or 70 percent interval is defined as average and indicates that some improvement is necessary. (3) Any course mean falling in the upper 80 percent, 90 percent, or 100 percent interval is defined as very good and indicates that very little if any improvement is necessary. This information could be provided in a computerized format, along with appropriate interpretive materials. These values could also be built into the computer program, to produce appropriate interpretive statements.

Once faculty members have been given comparative data and interpretive materials, they are ready to interpret results. Comparative interpretations result from normative data, and subjective interpretations result from reflections on what has taken place in the classroom that can be related to the comparative interpretations. Using this procedure, in addition to a careful reading of students' written comments (if available), each instructor should be able to generate diagnostic interpretations of instructional strengths and weaknesses in the course. If an instructor has results for two or more similar sections, then the ratings of one section may be compared to those of another, to determine what instructional behaviors may have led to higher comparative ratings in one section.

If faculty are unable to generate diagnostic interpretations, they may need to talk with department heads, deans, or instructional development specialists about the results—assuming, of course, that these individuals know how to interpret the results. If this approach still does not adequately identify the source of instructional difficulty, the instructor may want to consider other procedures (such as the use of additional diagnostic optional items, classroom visitation, and videotaping) in future evaluations.

After identifying strengths and weaknesses, the instructor can use the information to plan an improvement strategy. In some instances, the strategy may simply require minor modification of the course or the teaching method. In other instances, the strategy may require substantial time and resources on the part of the faculty member and the department. Through a process such as this one, instructors have been able to use student ratings to identify problems and rectify them. Obviously, the success or failure of such a venture rests solely with the instructor and his or her willingness to use the data provided.

If faculty members decide to submit copies of their results to their department heads or deans for rank, pay, and tenure considerations, then all appropriate interpretive materials should also be provided. Ideally, student-ratings results should be interpreted by someone with expertise in measurement and instructional development. Deans and department heads should be made aware of the need to use comparative data to interpret results, rather than relying on the more subjective and highly unreliable written and oral comments of students. Interpretations of student-ratings results may also be carried out by peer review triads, using several other assessments of instructional effectiveness, such as self-evaluation, quality of students' learning, and peer evaluation of content (Aleamoni, 1987).

Students' course and instructor evaluations should never be used alone in determining instructional effectiveness for rank, pay, and tenure decisions, since these data are not completely diagnostic of all elements in the instructional domain. How such data should be used in a comprehensive system of instructional evaluation, and how much weight they should carry, should be determined at the departmental level.

Faculty Evaluation and Faculty Development

Time and again, experience has shown that an evaluation system implemented without reference or connection to a faculty development program will generate greater amounts of anxiety and resistance among faculty than a system that is part of a larger faculty development and instructional improvement effort. Experience has also shown that faculty development programs, operated in isolation or without reference to faculty evaluation, tend to attract mainly faculty who least need these services.

Ideally, a faculty evaluation system should be an integral part of a larger evaluation and development program. For maximum benefit from these two programs, each element of the evaluation system should have a corresponding element in the development program. Thus, if the evaluation system is going to determine how well faculty teach courses or how frequently they publish scientific articles, there should be seminars, workshops, and instructional materials available to help them learn how to teach better or how to write manuscripts that are more likely to be accepted for publication. In short, the evaluation system should provide diagnostic information on the strengths and weaknesses that faculty members possess and then follow up with programs or materials to help them enhance their strengths and overcome their weaknesses.

Again, as a practical matter, the computerized report derived from student ratings should include written comments that not only highlight the major areas of concern but also provide information on where to seek assistance. For example, a computer printout could include a statement such as the following: "On the *testing and grading* section of the student-ratings form, the majority of the students (87%) indicated that your tests did not seem to relate well to the course objectives. The Office of Assessment and Professional Enrichment offers a seminar on test construction, which may be of some interest. Call 555-6432 for information about the next seminar." To be truly effective, a faculty evaluation program must work in concert with a faculty development program. Only in this way will both programs stand a reasonable chance of achieving their common goals: to improve instruction and enhance faculty performance.

References

Abrami, P. C., and Murphy, V. *A Catalogue of Systems for Student Evaluation of Instruction.* Montreal: Centre for Teaching and Learning, McGill University, 1980.

Aleamoni, L. M. "Student Ratings of Instruction." In J. Millman (ed.), *Handbook of Teacher Evaluation.* Newbury Park, Calif.: Sage, 1981.

Aleamoni, L. M. "Evaluating Instructional Effectiveness Can Be a Rewarding Experience." *Journal of Plant Disease,* 1987, 71, 377–379.

Aleamoni, L. M., and Stevens, J. J. *Arizona Course/Instructor Evaluation Questionnaire (CIEQ): Results-Interpretation Manual.* Tucson: Office of Instructional Research and Development, University of Arizona, 1986.

Arreola, R. A. "Establishing Successful Faculty Evaluation and Development Programs." In A. Smith (ed.), *Evaluating Faculty and Staff.* New Directions for Community Colleges, no. 41. San Francisco: Jossey-Bass, 1983.

Arreola, R. A. "The Role of Student Government in Faculty Evaluation." In L. M. Aleamoni (ed.), *Techniques for Evaluating and Improving Instruction.* New Directions for Teaching and Learning, no. 31. San Francisco: Jossey-Bass, 1987.

Derry, J. O. *The Cafeteria System: A New Approach to Course and Instructor Evaluation.* West Lafayette, Ind.: Purdue University, 1977.

Raoul A. Arreola is assistant dean for assessment and planning, University of Tennessee, Memphis.

Lawrence M. Aleamoni is professor of educational psychology at the University of Arizona.

Student ratings have been called many names, good and bad, but they do pose problems that have no easy solutions.

The Evaluation of Postsecondary Classroom Teaching: A Wicked Problem?

Philip McKnight

The purpose of this chapter is to consider the relevance of the "wicked problem" construct to colleges' and universities' efforts to provide accurate, fair, and useful information about faculty members' teaching performance. Those of us engaged in the design and administration of instructional evaluation programs in postsecondary education are familiar with the many problems that limit our ability to make evaluations more useful and valued. Budgetary constraints, support from faculty and administrators, and students' understanding of the process are all practical and political matters. Then there is the underlying issue of reification: we know that much is lost and distorted in the process of transforming complex concepts into numerical values. As Einstein is reputed to have remarked, everything should be made as simple as possible, but not simpler. This is one reason why most evaluation materials include a section for comments.

In responding to these problems, we have been assuming that they can be overcome or ameliorated with the help of such things as more time, more talent, greater dedication, more factor analyses, better optical scanning, and better instructions to those administering forms. If at first we are accepted only philosophically, as necessary to the activity of self-monitoring, surely we can come to earn credibility and respect for our demonstrable ability to improve instruction and, eventually, the academic growth of

I wish to thank Professor Steven Tripp for his help in bringing Rittel and Webber's "Wicked Problems" article to my attention and for his reactions to this chapter.

our ultimate client, the student. But what would happen if our assumption of inevitable improvement were challenged as not only weak but also inoperable? What if our fundamental belief in progress, a belief that has been with us since the Enlightenment, could not be sustained? We would be facing the possibility that we were operating from a dysfunctional, utopian viewpoint based on a positivistic cause-and-effect paradigm, wherein none of our variables would be modified in a way that could change the trajectory of our entire system.

Ten Properties of "Wicked Problems"

The discussion that follows briefly examines, from the perspective of classroom teaching evaluation, ten properties of "wicked problems" (Rittel and Webber, 1974) in the social sciences, problems that make it impossible to apply the classical paradigms of science and engineering to open social systems. These ten properties were proposed by Rittel and Webber (1973) in an article entitled "Dilemmas in a General Theory of Planning."

A "wicked problem" is an "aggressive" or "vicious" problem that, by comparison with a "benign" or "tame" problem, does not have a clear definition. With a "wicked problem," there are no criteria by which to tell if and when the problem has been solved. As noted, the classical paradigms of science and engineering are not applicable to the problems of open social systems. Likewise, the cognitive style of science and the working processes of engineering cannot be copied or mimicked in the social sciences. Social problems are resolved for individual situations, through political and social means, and not with any final authority. Therefore, they are subject to being solved again later, and often. "Wicked problems" have the following ten properties (Rittel and Webber, 1973):

1. There is no definitive information on the problem.
2. There is no way to know when to stop trying to solve the problem.
3. Solutions are not true or false, but rather bad or good.
4. There are no immediate and no ultimate tests of solutions.
5. Every solution is a one-shot operation because there is no opportunity to learn by trial and error, and so every attempt counts.
6. The problem does not have enumerable (or exhaustively describable) potential solutions, nor is there a well-described set of permissible operations that can be incorporated into solution plans.
7. The problem is essentially unique.
8. The problem can be considered a symptom of another problem.
9. A discrepancy that represents such a problem can be explained in numerous ways, and the choice of explanation determines the nature of the problem's resolution.
10. The problem solver has no right to be wrong.

To be sure, this chapter is not entirely congruent with the social programs (housing, welfare, highway planning) discussed by Rittel and Webber (1973, 1974). Designing a faculty evaluation program is not the same as designing an urban renewal program (although there are similarities in terms of the role of planning, desirable social outcomes, and the importance of establishing useful policies). Moreover, not all the problems of faculty evaluation are "wicked." The purpose of this chapter is to raise awareness, toward the goal of better understanding and responding to our unique difficulties. In sum, the "wicked problem" concept may be useful to us. For example, planning is an important aspect of our work, because of our concerns about outcomes and consequences for faculty as a result of our evaluation reports. Likewise, we cannot identify or describe all the influences on our work, let alone observe and trace their consequences for colleagues' personal and professional lives, and we deal with complex, ill-defined problems, as well as with the potential for mischief to our clients.

In the sections that follow, the ten properties of "wicked problems" are briefly considered for their relevance to the problem of faculty evaluation.

Property 1. With a "tame" problem, an exhaustive formulation of the needed outcome or solution can be constructed. Such a formulation is not possible for "wicked problems." According to Rittel and Webber (1973, p. 161), this poses a serious challenge because the understanding and solution of a problem are concomitant, and "to anticipate all questions (in order to anticipate all information required for resolution ahead of time), knowledge of all conceivable solutions is required."

With respect to evaluation of classroom teaching, it is impossible for us to identify all the solutions to the problems of valid questions, reliable administration, and procedures for collection and review, for a variety of class and subject types. Because we do not know the solutions, we cannot depend on the classical systems approach, with its distinct progressive phases. Instead, we must assume that our planning process is argumentative and that (tentative) solutions emerge and are later revised in a kind of dialectic process. If we do not recognize this limitation, we may not recognize the folly of naively (or arrogantly) assuming that we have identified the problem accurately and completely. Instead, we will be confidently noting what a good job we are doing defining a shapeless problem.

Property 2. With a "tame" problem, there are criteria to help us know when a solution has been found. With such problems as planning better evaluation programs, however, there is always room for improvement because there are no criteria for determining when a solution has been found (in this case, a totally valid and reliable system). How would we know, for example, if we had identified all types of teaching contexts or all variables involved with students' rating behavior?

Property 3. Solutions to "tame" problems can be assessed with conventionalized, objectified criteria, and such assessments can be independently evaluated: "Has the pesticide been eliminated from the processed fruit?" This question can be answered yes or no, unlike the question "Have we designed a valid survey for large, required lecture classes in sociology, taught by an assistant professor?" For one thing, answers would probably vary according to who was using the survey (students, peers, a committee on promotion and tenure), given different values and perspectives. Therefore, the answer would have to be "It depends. It is a good survey for group X but not, perhaps, for group Y."

Property 4. In contrast to "tame" problems' solutions, which can be assessed promptly, "wicked problem" solutions generate consequences over time, and it is difficult to assess the extent and importance of their impact. For example, if we start a peer evaluation program as a way of broadening the base of information and thus providing more complete teaching profiles, our action may have unseen repercussions for faculty morale. There is no way to account for those repercussions in advance and estimate some sort of cost-benefit ratio for our ideas. This dilemma may dampen enthusiasm for potentially useful innovations, lest we produce unacceptable costs for faculty.

Property 5. An attempt to evaluate teaching can be seen as each student's attempt to do so, or as the aggregate (the arithmetic mean of scores) of those individual attempts. Because class evaluations are normally done at the end of a term and are analyzed and returned even later, there are no second chances to reconvene the evaluating group (if, for example, it is found later on that inadequate or biased instructions were given to the students). To be sure, such information will be valuable in efforts to solve the general problem of teaching evaluations. For the faculty member, however, each evaluation is a one-shot operation.

Property 6. We cannot identify all the appropriate means of evaluating classroom teaching, because there are no criteria available to prove that all solutions to the problem of obtaining valid insights have been identified. We are comfortable with the assumption that students are the best sources of client feedback. Within any single class, however, do some students provide better insights than others, in a general way? Do those who attend all classes have better insights than those who show up only for exams? Do older, returning students have better insights? If so, are there limitations to their perspectives, which must be accounted for in our consideration of overall results? Or can we just assume that all the variable influences cancel one another out and give us the essential profile of a teacher?

In the end, we must limit our questions to a kind of generic profile of the teacher and to a standard list of assumptions about the clientele and the context (for example, a group of thirty to fifty undergraduate students in a lecture-size classroom, with the teacher standing in front and presenting a typical lecture). It would be interesting to develop a taxonomy of class formats and contexts, to see whether our assumption is valid.

Property 7. Rittel and Webber (1973) use the example of building a new subway in a city. Assuming conditions in that city to be similar to conditions in the San Francisco area when its system was constructed, they note that apparent similarities may mask unique aspects of both sites. The safest assumption, then, is that every situation is one of a kind. We can describe the different occasions of classroom evaluation in the same way. We can never be certain that the "particulars of the problem [for example, the classroom being evaluated] do not overrule its commonalities with other problems [that is, classes] already dealt with" (Rittel and Webber, 1973, p. 165).

Property 8. The search for a causal explanation of the discrepancy between an existing state of affairs (for example, less than desirable teaching performance) and what ought to exist is, for Rittel and Webber, the process of solving problems. "Wicked problems" present a situation in which the solution to one problem, through removal of its original and most obvious cause, reveals another, higher-level problem. This can be seen as similar to climbing a mountain: one reaches the top of one peak, only to find that it is merely a part of the total climb; the ultimate peak lies far ahead. Therefore, problems should be formulated at the highest level possible, to avoid addressing only symptoms. Nevertheless, addressing problems at too high a level may mean dealing with them too broadly and to generally. For classroom evaluation, the continuum ranges from construct validity to the goal of improving instruction as a means of educating students better.

Property 9. Poor instruction can be explained by several causes: classes that are too large (because of increasing enrollments during a time when no new faculty positions are being created), use of too many graduate students, faculty overload, poor high school preparation, and so on. Similarly, skewed grand means for a university sample can be explained by the volunteer effect, faculty dishonesty in culling out low ratings, poor rating scales, poor questions, and so on. According to Rittel and Webber (1973), there is no rule or procedure for determining the correct explanation or the correct consideration of an explanation.

Property 10. In the natural and physical sciences, it is assumed that solutions to problems are hypotheses about the true nature of things. These hypotheses cannot be proved; they can only be refuted, and if this happens, the solution is acceptable. In the social sciences (the world of "wicked problems"), refuted hypotheses are not so acceptable, because consequences can have significant effects on people. In our case, the effects would be on faculty members' careers and our own credibility. It appears that Rittel and Webber (1973), by assuming broad understanding of and sympathy for the scientific method, count on more tolerance from the scientific community's clients than may actually exist. Nevertheless, to the extent that the problems they address are actually research problems, their assumption may be accurate. We, by contrast, may be too pessimistic about our clients' reactions to our failed hypotheses. Perhaps it depends on the extent to which we build in checks and balances to provide security against our mistakes and chances to rectify them. For example, we may assume, incorrectly, that the same instructions read aloud to students will have a stabilizing effect on all classes, so that students' approaches toward an evaluation will all be the same.

In sum, it appears that the "wicked problem" construct is useful and should be considered carefully in planning for evaluation procedures. It seems clear that we are subject, in varying degrees, to the conditions and dilemmas represented by the ten properties of "wicked problems" reviewed here, and we must try to identify and control for their pernicious influence on our work.

Despite the recognized limitations posed by reification, and by the possibility (or probability) of the "givens" reflected in various aspects of the "wicked problem" scenario, we must act. We do not have the luxury of waiting for a perfect instrument or procedure to be developed. Personnel evaluation is not going to be suspended or ended just because it involves aspects that may be influenced in "wicked" ways. Without our work, evaluation will occur informally—that is, capriciously, without a system of checks and balances to counter gossip and hearsay. Even if we must admit some Faustian bargaining, we have to negotiate. More positively, we should remind ourselves that a fundamental value of our assumptions and theories is that they allow us to interpret events in intelligent ways, even if they cannot give us 100 percent predictability. It would also help to remember that perfection is a moving target.

References

Rittel, H.W.J., and Webber, M. M. "Dilemmas in a General Theory of Planning." *Policy Sciences,* 1973, *4,* 155–169.

Rittel, H.W.J., and Webber, M. M. "Wicked Problems." In N. Cross, D. Elliott, and R. Roy (eds.), *Man-Made Futures.* London: Hutchinson & Co., 1974.

Philip McKnight is professor of curriculum and instruction and of Western civilization at the University of Kansas. He also directs the university's Curriculum and Instruction Survey Program, which evaluates classroom teaching.

Student-ratings systems involve more than questionnaires, answer sheets, and reports of results. The reliability and validity of ratings systems can also be affected by the ethical decisions of those who evaluate and those who are evaluated.

Student Ratings of Instruction: Ethics and Practice

John C. Ory

From his survey of American colleges and universities, Seldin (1984) estimated that approximately 70 percent of institutions collect student ratings of instruction. Recent indicators suggest that this percentage has increased over the last five years. A survey of teaching-evaluation activities at forty large research universities (Ory and Parker, 1989) found that 100 percent of the institutions collected evaluation data that use student ratings. What started out as a student-initiated activity, aimed at helping students select courses more effectively, has become a powerful source of information that is consistently used by administrators to make personnel and program decisions.

How and why has the systematic collection of students' evaluations of instructors and their courses changed so much over the years? Many systems for collecting such ratings were originally developed by student government organizations, as early as the 1920s, to help students select professors and courses. Students developed the forms, and faculty could decide whether they wanted to distribute them to their classes. Student-initiated evaluation and voluntary faculty participation prevailed for the next three decades.

In the 1960s, students' demands for faculty accountability and course improvement changed the way student ratings were administered and used. Students began to ask for mandatory faculty participation. Administrators, in response to students' demands, agreed to consider extremely low ratings with respect to teaching assignments and, in a few cases, promotion and tenure. On some campuses, faculty committees became involved in developing questionnaire items and rating forms.

NEW DIRECTIONS FOR TEACHING AND LEARNING, no. 43, Fall 1990 © Jossey-Bass Inc., Publishers

In the 1970s, increased costs of higher education and mounting financial problems added to students' cries for accountability and led campus administrators to consider using systematically collected student ratings of instruction in the decision-making process. Nevertheless, few faculty members or administrators had much confidence that students' responses to student-developed surveys would provide a valid measure of teaching ability. Faculty and administrators had to be convinced, especially faculty. As a result, campus instructional services and evaluation offices became heavily involved in trying to understand the inner workings of student evaluations of teaching. Numerous research articles were published, addressing the reliability and validity of ratings, the proper way to construct rating items and forms, essential item content, and appropriate procedures for administering rating forms. Factor-analytic studies of results that identified dimensions of teaching ability flourished. There exist today over 1,300 articles and books dealing with research on student ratings of teaching (Cashin, 1988).

If the 1970s were the peak period for research on student ratings, the 1980s could be labeled the peak period for administrative use of student ratings. Financial problems forced administrators to make difficult personnel and program decisions based on evaluative information that met ethical and legal standards. As a result, many administrators, who were satisfied with the research supporting the validity and reliability of ratings, began to view student ratings as a useful and necessary indicator of professors' teaching ability. As Eble (1984, p. 177) explains, "Tangible measures of judgment get preference, not because they may be better, but because they afford written evidence that may stand up in court." The number of colleges and universities that require some or all faculty to collect student ratings seems to increase each year.

As the 1990s begin, we see most colleges and universities using student-ratings information for decisions about merit and promotion, while most faculty view the information as a valid but single indicator of teaching effectiveness. Over the last ten years, the collection of student ratings has evolved from a voluntary, student-initiated activity into a mandatory, or strongly encouraged, administrator-initiated endeavor. What major trend will appear in the next decade? Administrators' increasing demands for information have been accompanied by the placing of a higher value on results. Failure to be promoted and lower salaries can be the consequences for faculty who receive very low student ratings, even at many research universities.

So far, changes in instrumentation, data analysis, and reporting of results have kept pace with increases in the demand for and value of student-ratings results. What has not kept pace at most institutions are changes in administration procedures. There have been few if any modifications in the way faculty administer and collect student-ratings forms.

Typically, institutions follow an honor system that requires the instructor to give the rating forms to a student, ask the student to administer the forms after the instructor has left the room, and have the student send or deliver the forms to a campus office responsible for faculty evaluation. While such procedures are often required, seldom is there any institutional mechanism for monitoring instructors' (or, for that matter, students') adherence to the requirements. After approximately twenty years with the same administration procedures, our campus still has reported incidents of instructors administering forms as they walk around their classrooms or collecting and reading the evaluations before sending them to the campus office (and before final course grades are assigned).

Self-monitored procedures, combined with serious penalties for low ratings, have altered the behavior and sometimes comprised the ethics of some administrators, faculty, and students. Institutions that use student ratings in personnel decisions need to be aware of the consequences of this pressure to perform. Unethical behavior compromises the value and validity of student ratings; colleges and universities ought to develop procedures for dealing with undesirable and unethical behavior and preventing it.

To guide institutions in this effort, I will present nine scenarios of ethical situations that can occur or have occurred on college and university campuses. Each scenario is accompanied by a brief discussion of the ethical problems and by recommendations for preventing abuses.

Scenario 1

During the last week of the semester, Professor Adams invites her Psychology 200 class to her house for an end-of-course gathering. Approximately half the students taking the course attend the party and are entertained with plenty of home-cooked food and soft drinks. Toward the end of the party, Professor Adams distributes the university-required student-ratings forms and asks the students to place their completed forms on the dining-room table before they leave for the night.

Problems

This scenario illustrates several problems. Student ratings should be collected in the classroom, under normal conditions. A party atmosphere, whether at someone's house or in a classroom, may produce a positive bias that creates higher-than-expected ratings. Having students attend a social function to complete evaluation forms, at a time and place different from the normal class time and room, may discourage or prevent some students from participating and therefore produce a biased sample (partygoers may take school or ratings less seriously). Furthermore, the presence of the instructor while the forms are being completed may inhibit some students from being totally honest or from being somewhat critical, given their fear of reprisals.

Recommended Procedures

1. All student ratings should be collected in the classroom, during regular class hours and under normal circumstances.

2. Administering evaluation forms during the final exam is not recommended.

3. Faculty must not be present when rating forms are being completed.

4. Students and faculty need to be aware of university regulations for faculty to read prepared directions to their students before distribution of rating forms, to make sure students are informed about the purpose of student ratings and how the results will be used. It is also a good idea to print the directions in the student newspaper, distribute them to fraternities and sororities, and post them in the residence halls.

5. Students need some mechanism to inform (confidentially) the administration about instructors who fail to follow administrative regulations.

Scenario 2

Professor Jones has been concerned about being promoted and receiving tenure. She feels that her chances for promotion are much greater if she can balance her excellent research record with high student ratings of instruction. To accomplish this goal, she has collected student ratings in her elective classes only. To further enhance Professor Jones's chances for promotion, her department chair included only the courses with the highest ratings (he included ten of fifteen courses rated) when developing her promotion dossier.

Problems

Research (Braskamp, Brandenburg, and Ory, 1984; Feldman, 1978) indicates that courses taken as electives generally receive higher ratings than required courses do. By failing to administer student-ratings forms in all courses, required and elective, the professor presents an incomplete portrayal of her students' perceptions. The problem is magnified by her department chair's biased selection of only the highest-rated courses in the documents for promotion and tenure.

Recommended Procedures

1. For promotion and/or tenure decisions, assistant and associate professors should be required to provide evaluative data for each course taught at the institution, regardless of size, required or elective status, or content. A longitudinal profile, or summary of results over time, can be

used to evaluate growth and improvement. Administrators may want to require professors at all levels to collect student ratings each year, for use in annual salary decisions.

2. Administrators should be required to present complete course evaluations for decisions on promotion and tenure. If necessary, professors and administrators can include documentation explaining aberrant ratings (first-time course, instructor's illness).

Scenario 3

Before distributing student-ratings forms to his class in the spring, Dr. Ward spends fifteen minutes explaining the importance of student ratings and the need for students to complete the forms in an honest and sincere manner. He goes on to say how important this particular set of ratings is to him personally, because this is his sixth year at the university as an assistant professor. He explains that assistant professors are fired if they fail to receive tenure at the end of six years. He leaves the room, wishing the students the best of luck in the future and saying that he hopes to see them next year.

Problems
It would be inappropriate to label this behavior illegal and difficult to call it unethical. Perhaps the most appropriate adjective is *unprofessional*, because the professor's comments do cause a problem. The implied plea for help may pressure students to give ratings higher than those the professor deserves. Thus, the validity and reliability of the evaluations may be affected (Pasen, Frey, Menges, and Rath, 1978).

Recommended Procedures
No regulation can prevent a professor from offering this type of introduction, but administrators should discourage faculty from making these unsubtle comments. Institutions can take some solace, however: faculty can use this technique on only a few occasions, and one or two biased sets of ratings should have little impact on a six-year record of teaching (especially if other indicators of quality are included in the dossier, such as peer reviews and critiques of course materials).

Scenario 4

A history professor distributes student-ratings forms at the end of the term and asks a student to collect the completed forms, place them in the envelope provided, and deliver them to the campus evaluation office. After the professor leaves the room, a student begins to read the items aloud and describes his displeasure with the professor. A few more students begin to speak, and the class period evolves into a complaint session.

Problems

This may be the most perplexing ethical problem involving student ratings, because it is extremely difficult to prevent and detect. We want the rating of a faculty member's teaching performance to be an independent process. Peer pressure or the influence of a charismatic speaker can be detrimental.

While reading the instructions for completing the forms, faculty can remind students to refrain from discussing the rating process until after all the forms have been collected. Nevertheless, unless a student later speaks to the instructor, there is no way of knowing whether the class followed directions. Even then, what can an instructor do when informed that his or her class openly discussed the rating process?

Recommended Procedures

1. Directions read aloud by instructors should include a reminder that students should assign ratings independently.

2. In special circumstances, colleges and universities should consider granting instructors the right to withhold rating forms from final processing.

Scenario 5

Professor Wilson believes that he has excellent teaching ability and wants to make sure that it is reflected in his student ratings. At the end of each course, he administers the forms to his class and asks a student to return them to the campus evaluation office. When the student with the forms is leaving the classroom, Professor Wilson approaches and offers to deliver the envelope, since the evaluation office is in his building. With the forms in his possession, the professor returns to the office and "guarantees" his high ratings. First, he takes blank forms and darkens the bubbles on the machine-readable sheet, as though a student had completed the form. The number of blank forms depends on the number of students attending class on evaluation day and on the number of forms requested by the professor. Professor Wilson always requests slightly more forms than there are students in class, to ensure the availability of blank forms. For extra measure, he passes through the completed forms and erases marks for low ratings, replacing them with higher marks.

Problems

Fortunately, faculty groups are appalled when they hear of this type of behavior. Unfortunately, incidents like this have occurred, and without much fear of detection on the part of the instructor. Under normal conditions, the actions described in this scenario go undetected; it has taken strange circumstances to detect the few such cases reported to this author. Despite the fact that most professors are ethical, the honor system used at most institutions is inadequate for preventing unethical and unlawful behavior.

Recommended Procedures

1. As in scenario 1, faculty and students need to be aware of campus regulations for administering student-ratings forms.

2. Upon collection of the rating forms, the student who has been asked to help should indicate the number of completed and blank forms being placed into the envelope.

3. The student who collects the forms should sign the envelope and seal it in the presence of several classmates.

4. The envelope should be placed in a campus mailbox in the presence of several classmates. (Some campus offices require students to return completed forms in person.)

5. Institutions may want to consider refusing to process rating forms returned in unsealed envelopes. Experience suggests that such a policy would be extremely difficult to enforce, given the hundreds of courses evaluated and the number of student volunteers used each semester at large universities. If the problem is serious at a particular institution, however, such a policy may be worth enforcing. If a "no seal, no processing" rule is observed, faculty may need to remain after class and outside the classroom, to guarantee that students seal the envelopes.

Scenario 6

Before leaving the classroom, Professor Baker asks one of his students, Ruth, to collect the completed rating forms and send them through campus mail to the evaluation office. On the way to the mailbox, Ruth wonders how the class rated the professor. She opens the envelope and reads the evaluations. Disappointed by the low ratings of one of her best classes, Ruth erases a few low ratings and replaces them with higher marks. She returns the forms to the evaluation office, satisfied that she has corrected the injustice done by some of the less motivated, uninterested students.

Problems

Students and instructors alike can alter forms. In this scenario, the forms were altered by a student to improve the ratings, but they could also have been changed by a disgruntled student to lower the ratings. There is no controlling or knowing the motivation of a student who volunteers to collect the forms. An honor system for administering ratings relies on the proper behavior of instructors as well as students.

Recommended Procedures

The recommendations made in scenario 5, to prevent instructors from altering completed forms, should be followed to prevent students' alterations as well. Faculty members must feel confident that their rating forms are in reliable hands. The act of sealing the ratings envelopes in the presence of others may protect the rights of students (scenario 5) and faculty members.

Scenario 7

A math professor distributes the student-ratings forms to his class and returns to his desk at the front of the room. Propping his legs up on the desk, Dr. Janks begins to eat his lunch. As students leave the classroom, they stack the completed forms on the corner of his desk. With students still completing the forms, Dr. Janks picks up the stack of forms and begins to read the written comments on the back. The more he reads, the angrier he becomes over the "pettiness" of the comments. Who were these complainers? After the last student leaves, he attempts to analyze the handwriting in the negative comments and identify the complainers.

Problems

It is unfortunate that student ratings must be collected anonymously. Some instructors believe it is unfair to be evaluated on the basis of unattributed comments. Only after students graduate, however, can they be certain that they are free from any form of reprisal. Grades, letters of recommendation, and departmental awards are just some of the outcomes controlled by faculty. Students must be guaranteed anonymity to respond honestly. One indicator of the need for anonymity is the failure of many female students to respond to the demographic question regarding gender on rating forms administered in predominantly male classes.

The instructor in this scenario obviously made several mistakes. He affected the validity and reliability of his students' ratings by being present during completion of forms. He made matters worse by reading the forms in the presence of the students. The last students to finish probably wrote positive comments or none at all. The instructor's behavior not only affected the quality of students' ratings but may also have influenced the assignment of course grades. Further, an instructor may be a poor detective and may attribute a negative comment to the wrong student.

Recommended Procedures

1. Instructors should not be present when students are completing rating forms.

2. Instructors should not read results before assigning final course grades. The office responsible for returning results should not do so until final course grades have been posted.

3. Upon return of their rating results, instructors should be advised to refrain from attempting to identify respondents.

4. Students need a way to inform (confidentially) administrators of instructors who fail to follow administrative guidelines.

Scenario 8

Faculty members at Keebler College have the option of getting their rating results sent to their department chair. Dr. Simms is teaching a new course and is not interested in sharing these first-time ratings with the chair. When Dr. Simms's results are returned through the campus mail, the departmental secretary intercepts the envelope and makes a photocopy for the department chair, at his request. The chair wants to know how the new course is going.

Problems

One of the difficulties with the policy of requiring ratings for every course taught is that it inhibits the type of experimentation that can exist in new courses. A faculty evaluation system should be developed that does not penalize experimentation. A complete set of course ratings may be required for promotion and tenure, but faculty should have the right to withhold individual course results on a semester basis, in special circumstances. Evaluation systems that follow this policy should not be circumvented by nosy administrators.

Recommended Procedures

1. Instructors should have the right to identify the persons to whom the evaluation office should send copies of rating results.

2. The evaluation office and campus administrators must respect and honor the requests of faculty members.

Scenario 9

Several students complain to the chair of the biology department that their professor in Biology 100 altered his students' rating forms.

Problems

When confronted with the situation in this scenario, administrators must be prepared to deal with it fairly, following university regulations and federal and state laws. Most colleges and universities have a code of conduct that specifies inappropriate behavior or academic irregularities on the part of faculty and students and explains the consequences of such actions. Administrators confronted with accusations of unethical behavior involving student ratings need to know the appropriate procedures for making accusations, determining wrongdoing, and enforcing penalties. It is often difficult for students or faculty to prove wrongdoing in the administration and use of student ratings, but this difficulty should not cause administrators to refrain from pursuing complaints.

Experience has shown that administrators usually have one of two reactions when confronted with accusations of unethical behavior involving student ratings: administrators find the accusations so repulsive that they either dismiss them as absurd or want to act as judge and jury to punish wrongdoers. Unfortunately, neither behavior is desirable. What is desirable and necessary is that administrators take seriously any accusation of wrongdoing and handle it according to regulations.

Recommended Procedures

1. Institutions should have procedures for handling accusations of wrongdoing involving student ratings. The procedures need to specify appropriate mechanisms for making an accusation, determining wrongdoing, and imposing penalties.

2. Administrators need to follow regulations strictly when handling accusations of wrongdoing.

Twelve Recommended Procedures

These nine scenarios illustrate different types of unethical and, sometimes, unlawful behavior of students, faculty, and administrators involving the collection and use of student ratings. Since most institutions follow an honor system for administering student ratings, the honesty and ethics of individuals are paramount. Some kinds of dishonesty can be prevented by particular procedures within the honor system. Institutions need to evaluate their existing procedures and consider making changes that may prevent some of the behaviors described in this chapter.

Each scenario presented here includes one or more recommended procedures to discourage or prevent some types of unethical behavior. These recommendations are summarized in the following list:

1. All student-ratings forms should be administered in the classroom during regular class hours and under normal circumstances.
2. All students and faculty should be informed of procedures for administering student ratings.
3. The instructor should read directions (provided by the institution), see that forms are distributed, ask a student to collect the completed forms, and leave the classroom.
4. The directions should state the purposes and uses of the ratings, explain how to fill out the form, say when the instructor will have access to the results, ask students to respond honestly and fairly, assure confidentiality of responses, and remind students to work independently.
5. The student helper should collect the rating forms; place them in an envelope, along with a form that indicates the number of blank forms returned; sign and seal the envelope in the presence of several class-

mates; and, in the presence of several classmates, return the envelope to the evaluation office or place the envelope in a campus mailbox. Student helpers should also inform the faculty member and the evaluation office of any deviation from these procedures.

6. Faculty and student helpers should refrain from reading rating forms until results have been returned from the evaluation office, after course grades have been assigned.

7. Upon return of the results, instructors should refrain from attempting to identify respondents by analyzing handwriting or inspecting demographic information.

8. Assistant and associate professors should evaluate all their courses for inclusion in their portfolios. Faculty should have the option of releasing their rating results to departmental administrators on a semester basis. The evaluation office and departmental administrators need to respect the decisions made by instructors.

9. Administrators responsible for developing documents for promotion and tenure should include all available ratings. If necessary, the documentation can include information explaining aberrant ratings.

10. Students should have a mechanism to (confidentially) inform administrators of instructors who fail to follow procedures.

11. In special circumstances, faculty should have a mechanism to withhold ratings for a particular course from processing. Likewise, the institution should have a mechanism for withholding questionable or invalid data from disclosure, except to the instructor. Special circumstances may include students' failure to follow procedures. An institution may create an appeals committee to handle such cases.

12. Institutions should have procedures for handling accusations of unethical behavior, determining their occurrence, and enforcing penalties. Administrators must strictly follow regulations when handling accusations of wrongdoing.

The intent of this chapter is to encourage colleges and universities to review their procedures for administering and using student ratings of instruction and to make necessary modifications to prevent some of the unprofessional, unethical, and unlawful behavior that is occurring today. The purpose here is not to give the impression that the behaviors presented in these scenarios occur on a regular basis, or to diminish the validity and utility of student ratings. Collected and used properly (as they are in most situations), student ratings of instruction provide valuable information about a single dimension of teaching effectiveness—namely, students' perceptions of instructional quality. Student-ratings results are a necessary component of a comprehensive system for evaluating teaching effectiveness. Student ratings are data, however, and any data can be collected improperly and used inappropriately. Institutions that depend on student-ratings results must act responsibly to ensure their proper collection and use. If institutions fail to do so, unethical behavior may become a student-ratings trend in the 1990s.

References

Braskamp, L. A., Brandenburg, D. C., and Ory, J. C. *Evaluating Teaching Effectiveness.* Newbury Park, Calif.: Sage, 1984.

Cashin, W. E. *Student Ratings of Teaching: A Summary of the Research.* Manhattan: Center for Faculty Evaluation and Development, Kansas State University, 1988.

Eble, K. E. "New Directions in Faculty Evaluation." In P. Seldin (ed.), *Changing Practices in Faculty Evaluation: A Critical Assessment and Recommendations for Improvement.* San Francisco: Jossey-Bass, 1984.

Feldman, K. A. "Course Characteristics and College Students' Ratings of Their Teachers and Courses: What We Know and What We Don't." *Research in Higher Education,* 1978, 9, 199–242.

Ory, J., and Parker, S. "A Survey of Assessment Activities at Large Research Universities." *Research in Higher Education,* 1989, 30, 373–383.

Pasen, R. M., Frey, P. W., Menges, R. J., and Rath, G. "Different Administrative Directions and Student Ratings of Instruction: Cognitive Versus Affective Effects." *Research in Higher Education,* 1978, 9, 161–167.

Seldin, P. (ed.). *Changing Practices in Faculty Evaluation: A Critical Assessment and Recommendations for Improvement.* San Francisco: Jossey-Bass, 1984.

John C. Ory is director of the Office of Instructional Resources and associate professor of educational psychology at the University of Illinois, Urbana–Champaign.

Ratings do their work when they are used. Whether they work for or against the user is affected by how well the ratings system has been designed, as well as by the skills of its operators and users.

Communicating Student Ratings to Decision Makers: Design for Good Practice

Jennifer Franklin, Michael Theall

Anyone who uses student ratings of instruction as a measure of teaching performance or instructional quality should be aware of standards for good practice and other critical issues associated with ratings use. Faculty should be able to use ratings effectively as an assessment of the quality of the instruction they offer and as protection against the misuse of their own data. Administrators should be able to use ratings fairly and efficiently in performance appraisal without exposing themselves and their institutions to liability for misuse. We have become increasingly concerned that too many of those involved in applying ratings to the full range of evaluation activities, from questionnaire construction to decisions on promotion and tenure and consultation for teaching improvement, may not be aware enough of important ratings issues. We are convinced that providing safeguards against misuse of ratings data is an important task for those who plan or administer systems for collecting and disseminating student ratings of instruction. Our purpose in this chapter is dual: to discuss the problem of designing and implementing a critical component of ratings use—that is, methods for communicating ratings to those who use them—and, along the way, to demonstrate the usefulness of a systematic approach to identifying strategies or safeguards that can help prevent improper use of ratings results.

Over the past six years, we have been immersed in a full range of activities stemming from the establishment of a universitywide system for collecting student ratings of instruction. We designed, developed, implemented, routinely operated, and periodically evaluated a system for collecting ratings data and disseminating information to users. During this period, we collected ratings data from nearly 20,000 course sections. Providing consultation on evaluation-system development to other institutions gave us opportunities to explore similar activities in other settings. In the process of validating our instruments and the services we provide, we have conducted research probing such diverse issues of validity and reliability as relationships between the locus of students' performance attributions and important ratings variables (Theall, Franklin, and Ludlow, 1990); the knowledge, attitudes, and practices of ratings users in a variety of higher education settings (Franklin and Theall, 1989); and the relationship between instructors' grading practices and ratings variables.

From instructional systems technology we brought some praxiological habits, including the use of a common analytical method for developing instructional systems (see Romiszowski, 1981; Dick and Carey, 1985). Adapting this approach to the problem of constructing a large-scale processing and service system, we defined a strategy for development that required us to (1) identify and understand the needs underlying the development process, (2) define goals (desired outcomes) for the system, (3) analyze the information and skill requirements of rating-system participants, including staff and clients, (4) construct and operationally describe tasks performed by staff and clients in terms of the conditions and events instrumental to achieving the goals, (5) evaluate the performance of the system and its components and revise as necessary, and (6) ultimately evaluate the outcomes of the system, to characterize its effectiveness with respect to achieving its goals. We chose this approach, and we continue to apply it to our ongoing operations, so that we can consider our rating system as a whole, as well as account for each of its functional components.

Definitions

This chapter concerns the problems we encountered in the development process. Before we explore the particulars, however, we pause here to discuss the relationship between the process of communicating ratings to users and the question of how ratings are ultimately used.

Student ratings of instruction can be used to inform research and practice in a wide variety of instructional settings and applications. The many possible combinations of purposes, types of users, sources of information, and aspects of instructional quality demonstrate that rating systems are complex entities, even when they are small-scale operations.

Rating systems can be defined as more or less organized aggregations of processes intended to collect and disseminate student-ratings data, in order to provide information about instructional quality (especially teaching performance and course design) to users, who may include faculty, administrators, researchers in faculty development, evaluation, or institutional topics, and/or students, and who use inferences or hypotheses derived wholly or in part from ratings data to inform decisions, choices, or plans for action that are intended to maintain or improve the quality of instruction provided or received. This definition may be compulsively descriptive, but we hope it has the virtue of covering the *who, what, where,* and *why* in a field where writers and readers alike have frequently focused on the construction and validation of ratings questionnaires to the exclusion of other essential components.

For purposes of discussion in this chapter, whoever plans a system is at least a de facto *system designer;* those who are routinely responsible for providing ratings to others are *system operators. Client-user* or *user* refers to one who receives reports of ratings results from system operators. One person may assume more than one of these roles, or even all of them. Rating systems vary in scope, from a single user conducting an informal evaluation of a class to full-scale, campuswide, or even national ratings-data processing services.

Designing and Revising a Local Campuswide System

When we began our development project, we read as much of the literature on ratings as we could obtain. We found plenty of practical information about constructing, administering, and validating student-ratings questionnaires (Berk, 1979; Marsh, 1987; Weimer, Parrett, and Kerns, 1988; Scriven, 1989). We also found discussions of how ratings fit into larger evaluation processes, such as personnel decision making and teaching-improvement consultation (Centra, Froh, Gray, and Lambert, 1987; Erickson and Erickson, 1979). These sources tend to emphasize contexts for ratings use. For example, Miller (1987) notes that ratings used for personnel decision making should always be used in conjunction with other sources of information.

Although many researchers indicate the general relevance of their findings to practice, instructions or specific procedures for actually interpreting the effects of important variables (such as class size, required versus elective status of the course, or content area of the course) are not presented. Practitioners who have read Cranton and Smith (1986, p. 127) would be likely to agree that "one must be cautious in extending norms, even to an entire department," but how many readers have the skills or knowledge needed to make comparisons cautiously among sets of ratings? It is not even known what skills and knowledge are needed for using ratings. Meanwhile, other sources that debate the merits of such analytical methods as factorial weighting schemes (Marsh, 1987) presuppose the level of skill of the practitioner who would apply them (Abrami and d'Apollonia discuss the importance of dimensionality for interpreting and using ratings in Chapter Seven of this volume).

By combining what we learned from the literature, what we knew from our training and experience, and the advice of expert consultants, we were able to construct a large-scale rating system and to demonstrate the validity and reliability of the data we collected. We field-tested each process and procedure, increasing the complexity and scope of the services we offered over time and continuing to the present day.

By far the most difficult problem we encountered (aside from the stresses associated with garnering needed resources and the politics of providing data used in performance appraisal) was deciding how to report the results of ratings to faculty, administrators, and students. In the beginning, we approached the task as one of message design, deciding that printed reports should be readable, with lots of white space and clearly organized information. The available handbooks on ratings, particularly Doyle's (1975, 1983), gave useful suggestions about particular statistics we could use to summarize data. Accordingly, we tried to provide our clients with reports designed for legibility and appropriate analysis of their data.

Nevertheless, conversations with faculty and administrators during the years of development and implementation led increasingly to concern about what users were doing with the information we were providing. We saw that some departmental administrators, who routinely used ratings to make decisions about personnel, evaluation policy, and resource allocation, were not familiar enough with important ratings issues to make well-informed decisions. We regularly heard of personnel decisions that were made on the basis of a single course's ratings and of cases in which workload or difficulty were the deciding factors in such decisions, or in which mean scores, separated by tenths or even hundredths of a point, were accepted as valid indicators of individual differences in teaching performance. Each case is an example of poor ratings practice.

We received many requests from faculty for assistance in interpreting reports, and we discovered that our clients would not or could not use many of the instructions for interpretation that we had provided. Clearly stated disclaimers regarding the limitations of ratings data in particular circumstances appeared to have little effect on the inclination of some clients to use invalid or inadequate data. We found that the lack of resources for teaching improvement often made ratings data practically irrelevant to faculty development.

Designing a better reporting system became increasingly important. Using the systematic development paradigm, we began to look at the skill and informational needs of our clients. The difficulties we experienced looking for sources to inform the design and development of the reporting function led us to survey faculty, administrators, and teaching-improvement practitioners in five institutions, in order to probe their attitudes toward ratings and their familiarity with fundamental concepts of ratings practice (Franklin and Theall, 1989).

Our research findings, as well as anecdotal reports from many of our colleagues, suggest that many of those who routinely use ratings are liable to be seriously uninformed about critical issues. For example, among faculty respondents who reported using ratings for personnel decisions involving other faculty, nearly half were unable to identify likely sources of bias in ratings results, recognize standards for proper samples, or interpret commonly used descriptive statistics. Harris's (1990) study of evaluation instruments reinforces our concern. This does not surprise us, but neither does it condemn ratings users. Even though knowledge of ratings may be useful, other issues are the focus of their attention.

A great deal of scholarly attention has been paid to the validity and reliability of ratings as a measure of instructional quality (Cohen, 1981). Considerably less has been given to actual practice, other than the frequency of ratings use in postsecondary institutions. Utilization of ratings is one of the least often studied or discussed issues in the realm of ratings phenomena. There are very few reported observations of ratings users in action in personnel decision making or of the ways in which teaching-improvement consultants use ratings in interactions with their faculty clients. The latter have mainly investigated whether improvement is likely to occur when faculty are helped to interpret their ratings by skilled consultants (Aleamoni, 1978; Levinson-Rose and Menges, 1981; Cohen, 1980). Brinko (1990) takes a closer look at the way clients and consultants have interacted but does not investigate how ratings as such have been used. Similarly, there are few studies of ratings use by students or by those in institutional research.

To illustrate the need to consider the qualifications of ratings users, we offer the case of what to do with less than perfect data. Doyle (1989) rightly notes that academics are liable to "paralysis of analysis," overanalyzing data partly out a need to be safe. His statement that evaluators must work with data that may be less than perfect but that are still good enough reflects the general attitude of many of the most expert respondents in our survey groups. They share the recognition that ratings data are intrinsically both needed and imperfect. It is probably a safe assumption, however, that users who understand how and why data are imperfect are likely to be able to use them safely. Even given the inherently less than perfect nature of ratings data and the analytical inclinations of academics, the problem of unskilled users, making decisions based on invalid interpretations of ambiguous or frankly bad data, deserves attention. According to Thompson (1988, p. 217), "Bayes' Theorem shows that anything close to an accurate interpretation of the results of imperfect predictors is very elusive at the intuitive level. Indeed, empirical studies have shown that persons unfamiliar with conditional probability are quite poor at doing so [that is, interpreting ratings results] unless the situation is quite simple." It seems likely that the combination of less than perfect data with less than perfect users could quickly yield completely unacceptable practices, unless safeguards were in place to ensure that users knew how to recognize problems of validity and reliability, understood the inherent limitations of ratings data, and knew valid procedures for using ratings data in the contexts of summative and formative evaluation.

Whether the practices of those who operate rating systems or use ratings can stand close inspection has become open to question. It is hard to ignore the mounting anecdotal evidence of abuse. Our findings (Franklin and Theall, 1989), and the evidence that ratings use is on the increase, taken together, suggest that ratings malpractice, causing harm to individual careers and undermining institutional goals, deserves our attention.

Designing Systems for Use

Our fundamental assumption concerning the essential function of rating systems is that they should serve the goals of their users. Broadly stated, these goals involve maintaining or improving the quality of instruction provided by institutions or individuals. Accordingly, these goals are best served when rating systems provide useful information to those who make plans, decisions, and choices or take actions directed toward such goals. By examining the goals of ratings users and identifying the events that determine whether the goals can be achieved, we can learn what partici-pants in rating systems (operators and users) must be able to do to achieve those goals. We can also avoid the problems of setting unwanted conse-quences in motion.

Since the product of a rating system is information, the quality of the product depends on how it is communicated to decision makers and on whether it can be used to achieve their goals. We hope to make our case here by stating the obvious: ratings data are intended to be used, and so ratings results ought to be communicated to users in ways that best facilitate this use.

Communicating Ratings for Use

Although people speak of "using" ratings, data begin as responses, on optically scored answer sheets, to multiple-choice statements on question-naires. Quantitative summaries of raw data must be computed and then transformed into meaningful depictions of some aspect of instruction, course design, or individual teaching performance. How data are summa-rized influences both the scope and the content of interpretations. Users rely on interpretations of ratings as evidence when they form judgments of merit or worth. Interpretations of ratings data inform decisions, choices, or plans for action in matters ranging from personnel decision making to faculty development to teaching-improvement activities or such consumer-related issues as course selection.

Using ratings to obtain feedback from students on specific instructional behaviors, in order to inform efforts to improve teaching skills, is an example of ratings use in action. Using ratings to plan institutional strategies for allocating faculty development services is another. Even making negative personnel decisions, which include ratings as evidence of poor teaching performance, is an example (albeit Darwinian) of a strategy to improve instruction by removing all but the most highly rated teachers. The student who selects a course from a catalogue that shows course ratings can be seen as attempting to improve his or her own instructional experience in some way.

To this end, sooner or later in every rating system, the user receives (or constructs) some kind of report on students' responses. With the report in hand, the user forms a working hypothesis about what the ratings mean in terms of the user's own goals. This set of events is perhaps the most crucial in the ratings process, because here is where ratings do their work: at the point where value judgments are made, where attitudes are shaped, and where decisions are made. At the same time, this part of the process is most affected by the quality of the system as a whole because the validity of any judgment rests on the quality of the information the system provides.

The validity of inferences or interpretations should concern those who design and operate rating systems as much as validity and reliability of the instruments used to obtain the data. In a sense, the user is the last defense against bad practice, since the user makes the final decision about whether and how to use any data provided by the system. How use occurs ought to be a very important issue, one for which those who develop rating systems ought to be held accountable. Rating systems must empower users to recognize false or irrelevant information and avoid misconstruing valid and reliable information.

System Components

Taking a larger view of rating systems, it is useful for us to understand utilization in the context of the larger system and its more general events. Information about many of the processes associated with rating systems can be found in (or deduced from) the sources cited in nearly every chapter of this volume (see Chapter Three for a detailed guide).

We describe ratings processes in the context of three activities: establishing systems, operating systems, and using system products. (For the moment, we shall defer discussion of the first.)

Operating a rating system involves the following components:

- Obtaining data (selecting an instrument, where choices among validated instruments are required for services; administering it; performing whatever data-processing and data-management tasks are required for analysis)
- Analyzing data (selecting computational procedures for summarizing, quantifying, or enumerating; producing reports of responses—usually, but not necessarily, in a printed tabular report)
- Providing client-users with knowledge of results (face-to-face consultation; printed reports; telephone conversations; any other way of communicating results)
- Other tasks (those associated with data-processing systems and managing organizations; performing error checks and other quality-control measures, systematically and frequently enough to ensure accuracy in collecting and reporting data, budgeting, planning, and training).

How does a system get started, especially if it is complex? Even if one has a list of the processes required to operate a rating system, the list contains no indication of the things one must know or do to perform any of the tasks successfully. Without clear instructions, performing these tasks correctly would be difficult for anyone who was unfamiliar with the sources from which the list was derived. Moreover, without such information, it would be equally difficult for an observer to judge whether a task had been done successfully or at all. In small systems, the same person may be responsible for all these processes; in large, institutionwide systems, people who are never in contact with one another for any other purpose may perform parts of the overall system's work, with little idea of who is doing the rest or even of what the rest is.

We have deferred our discussion of establishing systems to demonstrate that rating systems are more than questionnaires or software. They may be complex entities that need careful planning and management. In other words, we want to demonstrate that the design of a rating system ultimately affects how successfully the system achieves its goals.

Here is a thorny issue, however. In the real world, rating systems are often not systematically designed and implemented. Certainly, an instructor-made questionnaire circulated strictly for obtaining informal feedback ("How am I doing?") requires less systematic consideration than does provision of the organizational resources needed to circulate a mandatory departmental or institutional rating form. Fundamental safeguards and standards for practice are easy to overlook when the system designer assumes that questionnaires and rating systems are synonymous. In the meantime, questionnaires may be disseminated, and data may be collected and analyzed, with little consideration of who is doing what and what the consequences may be.

If a mandate to provide rating services on any routine basis is established, the opportunity for careful system design exists. If the mandate itself is embedded in a systematically conceptualized plan for the evaluation of instruction, the system designer's task will be considerably helped. System designers must account for each developmental step in terms of how it affects the ultimate use of ratings data in various domains (personnel decision making, teaching improvement, course selection, research). Establishing a well-designed ratings system includes these components:

- Designing the system (conducting research, as necessary, including needs analysis for institution or clients; determining what kind of product or service is wanted and what type of system is needed; performing strategic planning: "drawing board" stage)
- Developing the system (developing and testing prototypes of system components, including questionnaires and data-collection procedures: "working models" stage)
- Implementing the system (putting the system in place; obtaining materials and equipment; training personnel; finalizing system schedules and procedures; building any necessary intraorganizational links, such as making arrangements to use the services of a centralized data-processing agency: "start-up" stage).

Once a ratings system has been established, these activities follow and continue:

- Managing or operating the system (conducting the routine business of administering questionnaires; collecting and analyzing data; reporting results to clients; performing monitoring tasks: "operations" stage)
- Evaluating the system (devising procedures for monitoring accuracy, performance meeting deadlines, utility to clients, and value, in terms of costs and benefits or other indices, in order to improve the design, development, implementation, or management components of the system: "evaluation-revision" cycle).

These processes of establishing a system and operating it are reiterative. Once a system is in place, the activities of improving existing services or creating new ones invoke new cycles of design, development, implementation, management, and evaluation. Additional functions (such as managing public relations, organizational development, and intraorganizational liaisons) lie in a gray zone between establishing and operating a system. We mention these mainly because they are often overlooked but are nevertheless important to the longevity of a rating system. The operating dynamics of the institution greatly affect these functions (see Birnbaum, 1988, for an important discussion of the ways in which colleges work).

Utilization: A Closer View of Tasks

Having identified the processes of establishing and operating ratings systems, we now have utilization to consider. Although many of the steps we have described ultimately affect utilization in some way, utilization begins with the user. Here are some of its essential processes:

- Receiving knowledge of ratings data (printed or verbal reports of analyses of data or even unprocessed, raw data)
- Evaluating quality of the report (establishing its accuracy, particularly course-listing information; determining the validity and reliability of the ratings data; establishing the adequacy of the report for the decision-making purpose at hand)
- Interpreting the report (constructing working hypotheses concerning the practical meaning of statistical summaries, in terms of the constructs about teaching or instruction that they are intended to represent; confirming the validity of any working hypotheses provided by the reporting system)
- Synthesizing interpretations of quantitative data with other sources of information to make judgments (making value judgments based on construing interpretations as evidence confirming or disconfirming some specified state of affairs; weighing the ratings evidence against explicit or tacit criteria for a valued state of affairs)
- Taking action based on results (applying judgments of merit or worth to decision making, planning, choosing, revising, recommending, advising, rewarding).

We noted earlier that ratings do their work when someone uses information for a purpose. Doyle (1979, p. 146) says that evaluation researchers "worry about four qualities of any data, including student evaluations: reliability, validity, generalizability, and skulduggery." To this we would add that practitioners who design or operate rating systems also must worry about comprehensibility and utility of the information they provide to clients. Recalling the literature, and looking over the processes described in the foregoing lists, we can deduce some of the conditions that are necessary before users will have information tailored to their own purposes.

First, ratings must be collected with validated instruments appropriate to the purposes of decision making. For example, in personnel decision making or course selection, the questionnaire may consist of from three to ten summary items, such as "this instructor compared with others," "overall amount learned," or "overall course quality." Composite scores, computed from factor-analyzed subscales, may also be used, but this is a more complicated process that requires expertise in measurement and evaluation.

For teaching improvement, the questionnaire will have twenty or more diagnostic, behaviorally descriptive items, such as "presented information at a rate I could follow" or "created an atmosphere of respect and trust," as well as any student demographic items that may explain results or contribute to planning for improvement, such as "I believe my background adequately prepared me for this course."

Second, data must be collected through procedures appropriate to the context in which results will be examined. For example, in personnel decision making, the instructor receives no knowledge of results until after grades are filed. In teaching improvement, the instructor personally administers the questionnaire and tabulates the data.

Third, analyses of data appropriate to the evaluation context must be performed. For example, standardized scores can be used to show comparisons between courses when personnel decision making is a goal. Course-rating catalogues should probably be restricted to descriptive statistics that demonstrate how many students said what.

Fourth, results must be presented to users in a format that is suitable for the purpose of decision making and that takes account of the skills and knowledge necessary for users to draw valid inferences from ratings data. For example, in personnel decision making, expert users require only appropriate tabulated, quantitatively summarized data, while novices are likely to need expanded narratives that explain the numbers and their relevance to important constructs in teaching and learning.

Fifth, users must be informed about appropriate procedures for applying interpretations of results to various decision-making processes. For example, in personnel decision making, the user knows that multiple sources of information about teaching performance are required. In teaching improvement, a single set of midterm ratings may be useful and valid.

Note that, despite the increasing detail, the activities still have not been sufficiently described to offer a fully operational guide to practice. It is not clear which things users must do and which must be done by the system. Appropriateness, validity, and effectiveness have not yet been operationally defined. The amount of information increases dramatically as each task is broken down into its components. We now take a closer look at the task of interpreting ratings, and we examine alternative strategies to ensure that users have valid interpretations when they act on ratings.

Operationally Describing Tasks

As system designers, our greatest concern, once we have established that we can provide valid and reliable data, should be to facilitate good practice in the use of ratings data in decision making. Selecting or constructing questionnaires, administering them, analyzing and interpreting results, and using interpretations to make decisions are processes that affect the quality of practice to an important extent. These processes can be described in terms of tasks. How these tasks are performed determines the quality of the system's product: the information it produces for decision-making users. Questions of who should have done what versus what actually happened can signal the quality of evaluation practice.

Once we understand the functional relationships among these events, and the conditions that predict success or failure, we can describe what must happen, in what circumstances, and by what standards it can be judged. Thus, we can identify performance problems in the system's components, including problems encountered by those who operate the system or use its products. When we can identify the skills and knowledge needed by practitioners and users, we can design the system to meet those needs. Once these processes have been identified and are understood, they can be described in terms of tasks, establishing who will do what, when, and how (that is, in what circumstances and to what criterion of precision).

The value of stating a ratings task as a behavior can be demonstrated in these two contrasting statements: "The instructor should administer the questionnaire correctly" versus "The instructor will (1) select a time for conducting evaluations that is during the last two weeks, is before finals, and is not during the same class session as any final examination; (2) designate a student monitor to distribute and collect materials, and instruct the monitor to strictly adhere to the instructions; (3) at the scheduled time, announce that the evaluation will be conducted, and state that the evaluation is important and deserves careful completion; (4) give the materials to the monitor, and leave the room until all evaluation materials have been collected by the monitor; (5) receive neither the completed evaluation packets nor any report of the results until after final grades have been submitted." The first statement is not very useful as a guide to practice. The second statement describes the task in operational terms that define the conditions most likely to elicit valid, reliable data. Constructing such a description not only helps us plan operations but also helps us clarify what we must communicate to our clients to ensure good results.

Many readers may recognize here what has become a routine part of designing or evaluating instructional systems: constructing behavioral objectives. This approach is limited in that it does not address larger issues, such as the value of the goals and objectives themselves, but it does provide a systematic approach to a complex set of phenomena, and it can be particularly useful when what will be evaluated has been designed with explicit goals and objectives in mind.

At this point, having placed the problem of communicating results in the context of the more general processes, and having taken a closer look at the problem of describing the processes in operational terms, as tasks, we begin to plan for designing the utilization process.

Designing Systems for Valid Interpretation of Results

The mechanics and style of interpreting ratings appear to vary dramatically across the domains of ratings use, particularly with respect to the role of quantitative information. It is our impression that many teaching consultants employ subjective, experientially based methods of dealing with information, while administrative decision makers may strive to construct empirically based (or empirical-looking) formulas to obtain clear-cut information or to reduce the appearance of subjectivity. Understanding how users operate should, ideally, influence how a rating system serves them, but considerable research will need to be conducted in this area before any useful generalizations will be available to designers who want to work with users' purposes in mind.

Still, there are some fundamental concepts for using numbers in decision making. To the degree that these concepts are ignored, interpretations of data become, at best, projective tests reflecting what the user already knows, believes, or perceives in the data. Treating tables of numbers like inkblots ("ratings by Rorschach") will cause decisions to be subjective and liable to error or even litigation.

Ratings data are similar in many respects to other survey data, and so ratings do not necessarily require especially esoteric or exotic statistical methods for analysis. Ratings are particularly subject to sampling problems, however, such as not having enough courses on which to base a comparison between two instructors and not involving enough students in rating each course section. Moreover, the fact that classes with fewer than thirty students are statistically small samples means that special statistical methods are required for some purposes. These sampling problems do not negate the value or reliability of student ratings, but we must never overlook such problems when we are using student ratings. Substantially different models for analysis are also required for various uses of the data. Given such problems, there are many opportunities for error in dealing with numbers. Three types of errors come to mind immediately.

The first involves interpretation of severely flawed data, with no recognition of the limitations imposed by problems in data collection, sampling, or analysis. This error can be compared to a Type I error in research—wrongly rejecting the null hypothesis—because it involves incorrectly interpreting the data and coming to an unwarranted conclusion. In this case, misinterpretation of statistics could lead to a decision favoring one instructor over another, when in fact the two instructors are not significantly different.

The second type of error occurs when, given adequate data, there is a failure to distinguish significant differences from insignificant differences. This error can be compared to a Type II error—failure to reject the null hypothesis—because the user does not realize that there is enough evidence to warrant a decision. In this case, failure to use data from available reports (assuming the reports to be complete, valid, reliable, and appropriate) may be prejudicial to an instructor whose performance had been outstanding but who, as a result of the error, is not appropriately rewarded or, worse, is penalized.

The third type of error occurs when, given significant differences, there is a failure to account for or correctly identify the sources of differences. This error combines the other two types and is caused by misunderstanding of the influences of relevant and irrelevant variables. In this case, a personal predisposition about teaching style, or the feeling that ratings are popularity contests, may lead a user to attribute negative meanings to good ratings, or to misinterpret the results of an item as negative evidence when the item is actually irrelevant and there is no quantitative justification for such a decision.

Any of these errors may render an interpretation entirely invalid. Even the most valid and reliable data may be misconstrued in these circumstances. Nevertheless, we can use these errors to explore how we can state what must happen operationally, in order to avoid them. If we can describe what the system should do and what the decision-making user should do, we will have a clearer idea of what the system designer can do to facilitate or ensure good practice among system operators and users.

How can we conceptualize the problem of ensuring that users do not make decisions or take actions that are based on invalid interpretations of data? In the following example, invalid interpretations are seen to result from either invalid or unreliable data or from lack of skill, knowledge, or necessary information on the part of the user. The strategy is to make sure that users either have or have access to sufficient skills and information to form valid hypotheses. Valid, reliable hypotheses are those interpretations of ratings data that knowledgeable, skilled users, with adequate information concerning the present data, would be likely either to produce or concur with.

Let us say that we state our goal in the following way: "The user will make decisions that are based only on valid, reliable hypotheses about the meaning of data." In this case, the user should receive or construct working hypotheses that do the following things:

- Take into account problems in measurement, sampling, or data collection and include any appropriate warnings or disclaimers regarding the suitability of the data for interpretation and use
- Do not attempt to account for differences between any results when they are statistically not significant (probably $< .05$)
- Disregard any significant differences that are merely artifacts of measurement (for example, small differences observed in huge samples, which can technically be significant but are unimportant)

- Account for any practically important, significant differences between results in terms of known, likely sources of systematic bias in ratings or reliably observed correlations, as well as in terms of relevant praxiological constructs about teaching or instruction.

The user should also refrain from constructing or acting on hypotheses that do not meet these conditions.

Since the operator provides the user with summaries of results, the role of the operator is crucial in ensuring that valid interpretations are possible and, better yet, likely. Some of the necessary conditions for operators can be inferred from the preceding list. Operators should ensure that all ratings data are sufficiently tested for validity and reliability before they are communicated to users; provide warnings to users concerning possible errors or problems in measurement; provide users with summaries of results only when the data meet the validity and reliability criteria appropriate to the decision-making purpose of the users; and provide users with valid interpretations or any necessary direct assistance for constructing them.

From this perspective, the system designer's task goes beyond testing the validity and reliability of all ratings instruments to be used in the system. The designer must also consider the tasks operators and users will perform and must do whatever is necessary to make users likely to refrain from making decisions based on invalid, unreliable data. The designer must be sure that procedures for testing and reporting the validity and reliability of data for each rated course and section are implemented. Furthermore, the designer must ensure that the user is either explicitly instructed or advised on procedures for determining validity and reliability and is informed of the necessity for using those procedures. For example, the designer can take measures to see that the user recognizes and rejects invalid or unreliable data, knows the criteria for validity and reliability, recognizes sources of sampling errors and other measurement errors, and accounts for known sources of error in any interpretation. This means that the designer must establish procedures to ensure that users are trained in, given instructions for, or provided with consultation on constructing hypotheses or else are provided with valid interpretations of ratings results and instructions for their use. The designer must also evaluate the quality of the decisions and actions of operators and users with respect to the quality of data and of the interpretations and revise the system as necessary.

Update on a Development Project

We do not mean that there are rigorous, specific, known methods for designing rating systems, but only that there are useful heuristics for dealing with analyzing processes and tasks in complex systems, heuristics that can be productively applied to the task of communicating ratings data or to any other aspect of rating-system design. We continue to find that the systematic approach we have described here is an essential tool for improving the services we offer.

We currently provide clients with specific report forms designed for use in teaching improvement, course selection, and personnel decision making. In our current ongoing system-development process, we have devised and disseminated report forms that meet the guidelines suggested in the literature. We have found, however, that many difficulties attend their use. As a result, we have entered a new development phase in which our objective is to learn more about the needs and skills of our decision-making users, in order to produce reports that will make their uses of ratings data as effective, efficient, and fair as possible.

During this stage, we plan to radically redesign the report that we provide to personnel decision makers by experimentally offering several alternative treatments for summarizing and explaining data. Each treatment will meet the general conditions established in the literature but will vary in format (graphic, numerical, narrative) and scope (embedded, individualized, interpretive comments versus general instructions). We will use interviews and surveys to probe the reactions of our users to these reports and will attempt to understand what characteristics of reports facilitate good practice.

Conclusion

We are convinced that those who develop and operate rating systems have an obligation to make the systems support good practice. It is not enough to provide valid, reliable information if the users are not prepared to make use of it. The rating process and rating systems are anything but simple. Individuals and institutions should be concerned about more than the wording of questionnaire items or how many points ratings will be worth in decisions on promotion and tenure.

We can assume that many of those who come to important ratings tasks will be relatively unfamiliar with at least some of the critical issues involved and will not have the time or even perceive the need to become qualified practitioners and users. The process we have employed to describe rating systems may seem tedious to some readers or merely commonsensical, despite its trappings of systems rhetoric. Our experience has convinced us, however, that the obvious is likely to be overlooked in the absence of tools for systematic development.

What can we do to improve practice, in these circumstances? Our feeling is that seeing the system in terms of its goals and what is needed to achieve them gives us an opportunity to discover a variety of alternative strategies for helping system developers, operators, and users do their various tasks. Allowing only skilled operators and users to participate in the system, or providing training, would certainly help establish good practice.

Because nearly everyone who is a client of rating systems is involved in other full-time work in a wide variety of academic disciplines, finding or training skilled users is often impractical. In fact, it is axiomatic that training is not always the only or even the best solution to every performance problem. Alternatives to training include providing detailed, step-by-step instructions ("job aids") and providing supervision and consultation from qualified peers or expert practitioners.

Rating systems themselves need periodic evaluation. Determining how effectively ratings are doing the jobs for which they are intended, and what other unplanned consequences attend their use, is essential to the integrity of any evaluation process but particularly to those that include consideration of ratings for personnel decision making. We need to understand current practice in operational terms. We cannot rely on having valid, reliable items, appropriate analysis, or useful reports if practitioners and users are unable to fully execute the tasks that underlie validity, reliability, appropriateness, or utility. It would be worse still if these persons were unaware of these requirements or did not accept their importance.

We regret having only scratched the surface of the problems of ratings use in our rush to make an important point: that the proper use of ratings should never be taken for granted, without strict consideration of the quality of the ratings data or the qualifications of users. For example, we barely mentioned tasks associated with policy and regulation, yet they are crucial to success. We totally omitted consideration of qualitative approaches to evaluating teaching and how they relate to ratings use. We even ignored one of our own fundamental assumptions: that without the opportunity for improvement of teaching skills, ratings are punitive.

Because the scope and complexity of rating systems will vary from site to site, in terms of who does what, how, and to what end, we are unlikely to find a single solution to improving practice. When we understand ratings systems as objectively described tasks, however, we can talk about what qualifications, training, or consultation people must have in order to perform the tasks effectively. Ultimately, we can also use this view to determine how well our rating systems are working, whether they are achieving their goals, and what we can do to improve them.

References

Aleamoni, L. M. "The Usefulness of Student Evaluations in Improving Teaching." *Instructional Service*, 1978, *1*, 95–105.

Berk, R. A. "The Construction of Rating Instruments for Faculty Evaluation." *Journal of Higher Education*, 1979, *50*, 650–669.

Birnbaum, R. *How Colleges Work: The Cybernetics of Academic Organization and Leadership.* San Francisco: Jossey-Bass, 1988.

Brinko, K. T. "Instructional Consultation with Feedback in Higher Education." *Journal of Higher Education,* 1990, *61,* 65–83.

Centra, J. A., Froh, R. C., Gray, P. J., and Lambert, L. M. *A Guide to Evaluating Teaching for Promotion and Tenure.* Syracuse, N.Y.: Center for Instructional Development, Syracuse University, 1987.

Cohen, P. A. "Effectiveness of Student-Rating Feedback for Improving College Instruction: A Meta-Analysis of Findings." *Research in Higher Education,* 1980, *13,* 321–341.

Cohen, P. A. "Student Ratings of Instruction and Achievement: A Meta-Analysis of Multisection Validity Studies." *Review of Educational Research,* 1981, *51,* 281–309.

Cranton, P. A., and Smith, R. A. "A New Look at the Effect of Course Characteristics on Student Ratings of Instruction." *American Educational Research Journal,* 1986, *23,* 117–128.

Dick, W., and Carey, L. *The Systematic Design of Instruction.* Glenview, Ill.: Scott, Foresman, 1985.

Doyle, K. O. *Student Evaluation of Instruction.* Lexington, Mass.: Heath, 1975.

Doyle, K. O. "Use of Student Evaluations in Faculty Personnel Decisions." In W. Becker and D. Lewis (eds.), *Academic Labor Productivity and Its Measurement in Higher Education.* Cambridge, Mass.: Ballinger Press, 1979.

Doyle, K. O. *Evaluating Teaching.* Lexington, Mass.: Heath, 1983.

Doyle, K. O. "Report on an Academic's Visit to Pragmatica." Paper presented at the annual meeting of the American Educational Research Association, San Francisco, 1989.

Erickson, G. R., and Erickson, B. L. "Improving College Teaching." *Journal of Higher Education,* 1979, *50,* 670–683.

Franklin, J., and Theall, M. "Who Reads Ratings: Knowledge, Attitudes, and Practices of Users of Student Ratings of Instruction." Paper presented at the annual meeting of the American Educational Research Association, San Francisco, 1989.

Harris, S. "Have Users Utilized Instrumentation Recommendations?" Paper presented at the annual meeting of the American Educational Research Association, Boston, 1990.

Levinson-Rose, J., and Menges, R. J. "Improving College Teaching: A Critical Review of Research." *Review of Educational Research,* 1981, *51,* 403–434.

Marsh, H. W. "Students' Evaluations of University Teaching: Research Findings, Methodological Issues, and Directions for Future Research." *International Journal of Educational Research,* 1987, *11,* 253–388.

Miller, R. I. *Evaluating Faculty for Promotion and Tenure.* San Francisco: Jossey-Bass, 1987.

Romiszowski, A. J. *Designing Instructional Systems: Decision Making in Course Planning and Instructional Design.* New York: Nichols, 1981.

Scriven, M. "The Design and Use of Forms for the Student Evaluation of Teaching." *Instructional Evaluation,* 1989, *10,* 1–13.

Seldin, P. *Changing Practices in Faculty Evaluation: A Critical Assessment and Recommendations for Improvement.* San Francisco: Jossey-Bass, 1984.

Theall, M., Franklin, J., and Ludlow, L. H. "Attributions and Retributions: Student Ratings and the Perceived Causes of Performance." Paper presented at the annual meeting of the American Educational Research Association, Boston, 1990.

Thompson, G. E. "Difficulties in Interpreting Course Evaluations: Some Bayesian Insights." *Research in Higher Education,* 1988, *28,* 217–222.

Weimer, M., Parrett, J. L., and Kerns, M. *How Am I Teaching? Forms and Activities for Acquiring Instructional Input.* Madison, Wis.: Magna Publications, 1988.

Jennifer Franklin is senior research associate at the Center for Applied Social Research and manager of the Office of Instructional Evaluation at Northeastern University.

Michael Theall is associate professor and director of the Center for Teaching and Learning at the School of Education, University of Alabama, Birmingham.

PART THREE

Research Perspectives

Teaching is a complex activity with many dimensions, which can be evaluated separately or globally. Global ratings are better for personnel decisions.

The Dimensionality of Ratings and Their Use in Personnel Decisions

Philip C. Abrami, Sylvia d'Apollonia

Student ratings of instructional effectiveness are used for many purposes. Students use ratings to select courses and instructors. Researchers use ratings to gather information on teaching and learning. Instructors use ratings for formative purposes—to gather information about particular strengths and weaknesses of a course and of their own teaching, for instructional improvement. Administrators use ratings for summative purposes— to make judgments about the quality of teaching for personnel decisions, such as promotion, tenure, contract renewal, and merit awards. This chapter discusses administrators' use of ratings for summative purposes.

Criticisms of Multidimensional Ratings

Multidimensional rating forms often contain specific items, which reflect a number of distinct constructs (dimensions) of instructional effectiveness, as well as a few global items reflecting students' overall evaluation. For example, global items useful for summative purposes include the following: How would you rate the instructor in overall ability? How would you rate the quality of this course? How much have you learned in this course, compared to others? The results of such rating forms are often factor-analyzed, yielding factor scores for subsets of intercorrelated items. Typical factors that are generated are *Skill* (the instructor has a good command of the subject matter), *Rapport* (the instructor is friendly), *Structure* (the instructor uses class time well), *Difficulty* (the instructor assigned difficult reading), *Interaction* (the instructor facilitates class discussion), and *Feedback* (the instructor keeps students informed of their progress).

NEW DIRECTIONS FOR TEACHING AND LEARNING, no. 43, Fall 1990 © Jossey-Bass Inc., Publishers

Abrami (1989a; see also Abrami, 1985, 1988, 1989b) argues that when student ratings of instruction are used for summative purposes, decisions should be based on the data from several global ratings or on a carefully weighted average of the factor scores, instead of on several separate factor scores. Abrami (1989a) acknowledges that teaching effectiveness has many components, but he gives several reasons why multidimensional rating forms should not be used for personnel decisions. In general, these reasons reflect the failure of the existing student-ratings systems, when compared to composite scores based on global ratings, to provide the best evidence for summative decisions on teaching.

First, the content validity of specific items and of some factors that they comprise is questionable when ratings are used across a wide variety of courses, instructors, students, and settings. For example, the appropriateness of items on Rapport and Interaction is different in large classes and in small ones, in discussion or studio classes and in lectures. For a multidimensional rating form to have content validity, its items must elicit a representative sample of students' descriptions from the relevant domains of the instructor's behavior. A rating form should not contain too many items assessing one sort of behavior and too few assessing another. Moreover, a rating form should contain items equally relevant to each of the instructional situations for which it was designed. Of what relevance are the items "Students were encouraged to participate in class discussion" and "Instructor was friendly toward individual students" in classes with very high enrollments, especially by comparison with small classes? Imagine an instructor who encourages each student to participate when class size is over one hundred. Instructional situations vary so much that it is wrong to suggest that all instructional characteristics are equally relevant, and yet this assumption underlies every universal, multidimensional rating form where these factors appear.

Cohen's (1981) quantitative review of multisection validity studies suggests a second reason for the failure of existing systems. His review shows that many rating factors have lower correlations with student learning (Rapport = .31, Interaction = .22, Feedback = .31, Evaluation = .23) or near 0 correlations with student learning (Difficulty = -.02) by comparison with Overall Course (.47) and Overall Instructor (.43) correlations with learning. Thus, the construct validity of some rating factors is not strongly supported by research on ratings and on teacher-produced student achievement.

A third reason for failure is that much less is known about the generalizability of specific rating factors than about global ratings—specifically, less is known about the construct validity of rating factors (that is, their ability to measure effective teaching) than about global ratings under a variety of conditions that involve the course, the instructor, students, and the setting. Furthermore, the validity of the specific factors can be expected to vary across situations, since the factors are often reasonably independent of one another. The knowledge that one rating factor is uninfluenced by a biasing characteristic offers little assurance about the absence of the bias in other factors (see Abrami, d'Apollonia, and Cohen, 1990).

Finally, one cannot expect untrained administrators or nonexperts in evaluation, attempting to arrive at a single decision about the quality of an instructor's teaching, to properly weigh the information provided by factor scores (Franklin and Theall, 1989). This is particularly troublesome when comparative judgments about teaching are made. One cannot expect administrators to have the expertise of instructional evaluators, nor are there precise and defensible procedures for synthesizing the information from factor scores. Experience suggests that administrators weigh factor scores equally or look for particularly strong or weak areas of teaching. It would be disappointing to learn that a faculty member was denied tenure because of low student ratings on Difficulty when such ratings are almost totally uncorrelated with students' learning.

Are Rating Factors Uniform?

An underlying assumption of the multidimensional approach to the evaluation of instruction is that the characteristics of effective teaching are substantially invariable (Marsh and Hocevar, 1984). It is generally assumed that the qualities important to effective teaching should not vary from course to course, from department to department, or from university to university. In other words, researchers have largely sought to find common aspects of teaching that do not change from course to course. Unfortunately, however, in their desire to find these common factors, researchers may have underestimated or ignored the possibility that effective teaching may be situation-specific.

The assumption of common teaching qualities is one basis on which the factor analysis of multi-item rating forms proceeds. Factor analysis is the analysis of responses across instructors, courses, departments, and so on, to identify two or more subsets of items that are interrelated. Thus, items that share common variance constitute a factor: students' responses to one item predict their responses to other items in that factor. Furthermore, the results of each factor analysis can be replicated across different disciplines and universities or even by comparison of students' ratings with instructors' self-ratings (Marsh, 1987). Nevertheless, the replicability across situations from one multi-item form does not guarantee replicability across forms. If there were replicability across forms, one would expect the same teaching qualities to emerge on each multidimensional rating form; there would not be substantial variability across forms in the factors of effective teaching that these forms assess. Moreover, the relative type and proportion of items representing these factors would also not vary across forms—that is, are the factors from evaluation instrument A similar to those from instrument B? If they are not similar, is it reasonable to suggest that the factors of effective teaching are known and invariable? We think not.

To assess the uniformity of existing multidimensional rating forms, we decided to categorize different rating items by using a common scheme. We also selected for analysis only findings from studies on the validity of student ratings for predicting teacher-produced differences in students' learning. To date, our analysis of this literature includes a critique of several quantitative syntheses of the literature (Abrami, Cohen, and d'Apollonia, 1988), as well as the nomological coding and analysis of the important features of the primary studies (Abrami, d'Apollonia, and Cohen, 1990).

Identification of Studies

Broadly speaking, the validity of student ratings may be approached from two fundamentally different perspectives. From one point of view, student ratings are valid if they accurately reflect students' opinions about the quality of instruction, regardless of whether the ratings reflect what students learn—that is, the satisfaction of students with instruction is considered worth knowing, since students are consumers of the teaching process. Student ratings are seldom criticized as measures of students' satisfaction with instruction. From the second viewpoint, student ratings are valid if they accurately reflect instructional effectiveness—that is, students' beliefs about the quality of instruction are hypothesized to reflect the processes of teaching (for example, what instructors do when they teach) or the impact of instructors on the desired products of instruction (for example, the amount students learn) or both the processes and the products of instruction. Student ratings are often criticized as measures of instructional effectiveness.

Student-ratings factors, such as Group Interaction and Individual Rapport are sometimes validated as measures of instructional processes, if it can be shown that these factors are correlated with students' overall judgments of effectiveness (Feldman, 1976) and with the judgments of colleagues, former students, administrators, and external observers (Feldman, 1989). Ratings as measures of process are also validated if it can be shown that students form their judgments on the basis of what is taught and are uninfluenced by their own characteristics or by characteristics extraneous to instruction (Feldman, 1977, 1978, 1979).

Nevertheless, using student ratings to consider instructional processes has a serious shortcoming: the failure to establish how these processes measure effectiveness, without ultimately resorting to product or outcome measures. Consequently, we shall concentrate here on considering the validity of ratings for assessing the products of effective instruction.

In the multisection validation design, researchers correlate mean student ratings with mean student achievement on a common examination from multiple sections of a college course. This is a validity coefficient. A large, positive value of the coefficient is taken as evidence of rating validity. To date, more than forty studies have used the multisection design to address the validity of student ratings. The design has several features that make its internal validity high. Using class-section means, rather than students (or students pooled across classes), as the unit of analysis emphasizes the instructor's effects on ratings and achievement. In many of these studies, furthermore, sectional differences in students' characteristics were controlled experimentally, via random assignment, or statistically, via ability pretests. Similarly, sectional differences in setting effects were often minimized with the use of a common syllabus, a common textbook, similar class size, and so on. Finally, the effect of the instructor's grading standards was reduced by the use of a common examination for all sections. Therefore, the design minimizes the extent to which the correlation of student ratings with achievement can be explained by factors other than the instructor's influence.

One of the strongest features of the design is that the validity criterion—mean sectional examination performance—is relatively high in external validity. Examination scores are a direct and important measure of one of the products of effective instruction and are designed not only for assessing what students have learned of the course material but also for assigning grades.

Studies Coded

Abrami, Cohen, and d'Apollonia (1988) found forty-four studies of student-ratings validity that met five criteria. (1) The data came from actual classes and not from experimental analogues, such as the Doctor Fox studies (Abrami, Leventhal, and Perry, 1982); (2) courses were taught at the postsecondary level, and no validation studies from high school classes were included; (3) correlations were computed on the basis of class-section means (which best represent instructors' influences) and were not based on individual students or on pooled students as the units of analysis; (4) all the studies used validity coefficients computed across multiple sections of the same course; and (5) only studies with the criterion of instructional effectiveness (students' achievement on course examinations) across course sections were included.

Coding System

Feldman (1976) has developed a classification system for sorting items and factors from different student-ratings forms into nineteen dimensions. These dimensions are designed to capture the range of items and factors found on multidimensional rating forms. In subsequent work (Feldman, 1983, 1984), this system was revised, and two dimensions were added. To these twenty-one dimensions we have added three others: overall course, overall instructor, and a miscellaneous category. The miscellaneous category includes items that do not fit into any other dimension. To derive working definitions of these twenty-one dimensions, we first listed, by dimension, all the examples that Feldman (1976) presents. After our initial review of these items, during which we clarified ambiguities, we developed the definitions that we offer here (examples of items from the multisection validity studies fitting these dimensions are presented in Exhibit 1).

Exhibit 1. Examples of Items Used in Multisection Validity Studies, Categorized into Dimensions

Stimulation of Interest
1. The instructor put material across in an interesting way.
2. The teacher stimulated the intellectual curiosity of the students.
3. I was attentive in class.

Enthusiasm
1. The instructor showed boredom for teaching this class.
2. The instructor seemed to be interested in teaching.
3. The instructor demonstrated dynamism and enthusiasm for the subject.

Knowledge of the Subject
1. The instructor had a thorough knowledge of the subject matter.
2. The instructor accepted or used inaccurate information.
3. The instructor was aware of scientific methods.

Intellectual Expansiveness
1. The instructor exhibited a high degree of cultural attainment.
2. The instructor was admired for great intelligence.
3. The instructor has several college degrees.

Preparation and Organization of the Course
1. Lectures were well planned for each class.
2. Each class period was carefully planned.
3. The instructor delivered orderly material.

Clarity and Understandableness
1. The instructor summarized or emphasized major points in lectures or discussions.
2. Rate the extent to which the instructor was successful in explaining the course material.
3. The instructor explained clearly, and the explanations were to the point.

Elocutionary Skills
1. The instructor did not speak clearly.
2. Rate the instructor's voice and mannerisms.
3. The instructor was clear and audible.

Exhibit 1. (continued)

Class Level and Progress
1. The instructor seemed to know when students did not understand the material.
2. The instructor was aware of when students failed to keep up with the presentation of material in class.
3. The instructor changed approaches to meet new situations.

Clarity of Course Objectives
1. Rate the degree to which the objectives of the course were clarified and discussed.
2. The instructor's objectives for the course were clear.
3. The instructor told students how they would be evaluated in the course.

Relevance and Value of Course Materials
1. Assignments were uninteresting and were of little or no value.
2. Rate the extent to which the text was a useful part of the course.
3. The instructor called often on relevant personal experiences in teaching the subject.

Relevance and Usefulness of Supplementary Materials
1. Overall, I would rate the supplementary readings as _____ .
2. The instructor provided a variety of activities in class and used a variety of media—slides, films, projections, drawings, and outside resources.

Workload
1. The student had to work hard in the course.
2. The instructor demanded more than I could do.
3. I have found the material in this course to be inherently difficult.

Perceived Outcome
1. In this class, I developed skills and knowledge directly related to my plans after I finish college.
2. The course increased my general knowledge.
3. I can organize and reorganize the elements of a complex problem to produce a pattern not clearly there before.

Fairness of Evaluation
1. Examinations reflected important aspects of the course.
2. Rate the instructor on fair and impartial grading.
3. Rate the instructor's grading of experiments and reports.

Classroom Management
1. The students had a voice in deciding how we did what was done.
2. The teacher made it clear that students would have little choice in how their achievement would be assessed.
3. The instructor encouraged class members to work as a team.

Personality Characteristics
1. Rate the instructor's sense of proportion and sense of humor.
2. Rate the extent to which the instructor was easygoing and informal.
3. The instructor was crabby.

Exhibit 1. (*continued*)

Feedback
1. The instructor made helpful comments on papers or exams.
2. Rate the instructor's returning of daily quizzes and tests, and contrast not returning them to returning them with full explanation of errors.
3. The instructor expressed appreciation when one of us did a good job.

Encouragement of Discussion and Diversity of Opinions
1. In this class, we tried to understand points of view that differed from our own.
2. Students interacted with other students.
3. The instructor encouraged class discussion.

Intellectual Challenge and Encouragement of Independent Thought
1. This course challenged me intellectually.
2. The instructor raised challenging questions.
3. The teacher asked open-ended questions.

Concern and Respect for Students
1. The instructor established good rapport in a friendly and supportive way.
2. Was the instructor considerate of and interested in the students?
3. The instructor was friendly.

Availability and Helpfulness
1. The students were able to get personal help.
2. The instructor established and kept office hours for individual conferences.
3. The instructor was not readily available for consultation, by appointment or otherwise.

Overall Course
1. Rate the course.
2. Rate the overall effectiveness of the course.
3. I enjoyed every moment of the course.

Overall Instructor
1. How would you rate your teacher in general?
2. Grade the instructor.
3. How much did you like your instructor as a teacher?

Miscellaneous Items
1. Rate the suitability of the class size.
2. Rate the instructor's care of communal apparatus.
3. The students in the class were friendly.

Dimension 1: Stimulation of Interest. The students are evaluating the extent to which the instructor captured and maintained their attention by such means as stimulating their interest in the course, arousing their intellectual curiosity, and so on.

Dimension 2: Enthusiasm. The students are evaluating the extent to which the instructor communicated his or her enthusiasm, either for the subject or for teaching.

Dimension 3: Knowledge of the Subject. The students are evaluating the extent to which the instructor demonstrated his or her knowledge of the subject matter.

Dimension 4: Intellectual Expansiveness. The students are evaluating the extent to which the instructor demonstrated his or her breadth of knowledge and cultural attainment, beyond the immediate subject matter.

Dimension 5: Preparation and Organization of the Course. The students are evaluating the extent to which the instructor prepared himself or herself for instruction.

Dimension 6: Clarity and Understandableness. The students are evaluating the extent to which the instructor delivered clear, concise, comprehensible material.

Dimension 7: Elocutionary Skills. The students are evaluating the extent to which the instructor demonstrated skill in vocal delivery.

Dimension 8: Class Level and Progress. The students are evaluating the extent to which the instructor was concerned with and able to monitor students' learning.

Dimension 9: Clarity of Course Objectives. The students are evaluating the extent to which the instructor communicated and met clear course objectives and criteria.

Dimension 10: Relevance and Value of Course Materials. The students are evaluating the extent to which the instructor communicated the value and relevance of course materials, including textbooks, assignments, and so on.

Dimension 11: Relevance and Usefulness of Supplementary Materials. The students are evaluating the degree to which the instructor's use of supplementary materials (film, audiovisual aids, and so on) was relevant and useful.

Dimension 12: Workload. The students are evaluating the amount of work required by the course and the appropriateness of the workload.

Dimension 13: Perceived Outcome. The students are evaluating specific skills they have acquired as a result of having taken the course.

Dimension 14: Fairness of Evaluation. The students are evaluating the extent to which the instructor provided appropriate, impartial, and effective evaluation.

Dimension 15: Classroom Management. The students are evaluating the extent to which the instructor managed the classroom environment, including the type of teaching style exhibited by the instructor.

Dimension 16: Personality Characteristics. The students are evaluating the personal characteristics of the instructor, without reference to their impact on teaching or on the class.

Dimension 17: Feedback. The students are evaluating the extent to which the instructor provided appropriate and effective feedback.

Dimension 18: Encouragement of Discussion and Diversity of Opinions. The students are evaluating the extent to which the instructor encouraged discussion and questions and maintained an open, tolerant atmosphere.

Dimension 19: Intellectual Challenge and Encouragement of Independent Thought. The students are evaluating the extent to which the instructor stimulated them intellectually and encouraged higher-order learning, such as independent thinking and problem solving.

Dimension 20: Concern and Respect for Students. The students are evaluating the extent to which the instructor was concerned about and respected students—that is, the extent to which the instructor had positive social interactions with students.

Dimension 21: Availability and Helpfulness. The students are evaluating the extent to which the instructor was available and helpful outside the classroom.

Category 22: Overall Course. The students are evaluating the overall worth of the course.

Category 23: Overall Instructor. The students are evaluating the overall effectiveness of the instructor.

Category 24: Miscellaneous Items. This category is a repository for items that we were unable to categorize in the other dimensions.

Difficulties

We encountered some difficulty categorizing certain items, since some dimensions encompass the instructional process, while others encompass the instructional product for the same instructional activity. For example, items referring to the instructor's ability to engage the student are categorized in dimension 1, while items referring to the student's stimulated curiosity and interest are categorized in dimensions 13 and 19. Items referring to the instructor's preparation and organization are categorized in dimension 5, while items referring to the clarity and logic of the resulting presentation are categorized in dimension 6. Items referring to the instructor's communication of grading criteria are categorized in dimension 9, while the student's knowledge of the grading criteria is categorized in dimension 14. It is often difficult to decide whether items are stressing the process or the product of instruction. A rater's categorization of such items may reflect the rater's philosophy, rather than any objective quality of the item.

Coding Procedures

Two graduate students coded all the items in the studies. When the items from a rating form were not in a particular validity study, they were sought from other sources. When these sources were not available, coding proceeded on the basis of available information (for example, factor labels, other reviews). Interrater reliability was .93 (Cohen's "kappa"). This high reliability probably reflects both establishment of definitions for the dimensions and extensive training on examples before coding.

For each of the validity coefficients reported in the literature, the coders recorded the number of items used by the primary researchers in the twenty-four dimensions. For example, if a validity coefficient was based on a five-item factor, three items might represent dimension 3, one item dimension 18, and one item dimension 19. Thus were we able to determine the number of items (N) representing each dimension, which appeared in the rating forms used in the forty-three studies. A high N meant the dimension appeared frequently. The maximum N was 154 (the number of study findings).

We then computed the uniformity index (UI), which is a measure of the unidimensionality of reported validity coefficients across rating forms. A high UI meant that the validity coefficients tended to represent a single dimension. Standard deviation for the UI was also computed, as a measure of the variability in the number of dimensions among the rating forms used to generate the validity coefficients.

Studies often report more than a single set of validity coefficients. For example, one study may report validity coefficients for chemistry courses separately from psychology courses; even though data may have come from a single study, we treated these results as two findings. Treating the finding, not the study, as the unit of analysis increases the dependence, or correlation, of the results. This dependence works against the possibility of detecting that items from different forms are diverse, because the same rating forms are used repeatedly.

Results of Uniformity Analysis

W: found a total of 752 validity coefficients distributed among 154 findings. Table 1 presents the descriptive statistics for the uniformity analysis of the 154 study findings. First, all twenty-one dimensions, the two overall categories, and the miscellaneous category are represented in the student-ratings forms used in the validity study, but the frequency with which the dimensions appear varies. The most frequent dimensions (Clarity and Understandableness, and Overall Course) appeared in more than two-thirds of the findings. In contrast, the least frequent dimensions (Supplementary Materials and Instructor's Enthusiasm) appeared in fewer than one-fifth of the findings.

Second, except for the global rating categories (Overall Course and Overall Instructor), the uniformity indices are small, indicating that the reported validity coefficients (based, in most cases, on factor scores) are multidimensional. In addition, the standard deviations of these uniformity indices are quite high (on the order of 0.12 to 0.45). These large standard deviations indicate that there is little consistency in the dimensions among the rating forms in the literature.

The following example may clarify these points. Of the forty-three validity coefficients representing correlations of student achievement with

Table 1. Uniformity Analysis (UI) of Student-Ratings Forms (N = 154 Study Findings)

Dimension	N	UI
Stimulation of interest	88	0.25
Enthusiasm	30	0.23
Knowledge of the subject	43	0.36
Intellectual expansiveness	35	0.11
Preparation and organization	89	0.33
Clarity and understandableness	112	0.30
Elocutionary skills	54	0.13
Class level and progress	76	0.20
Clarity of course objectives	68	0.25
Relevance and value of materials	46	0.38
Supplementary materials	26	0.36
Workload	84	0.45
Perceived outcome	75	0.47
Fairness of evaluation	69	0.39
Classroom management	79	0.25
Personality characteristics	54	0.25
Feedback	66	0.24
Encouragement of discussion	90	0.35
Intellectual challenge	35	0.24
Concern and respect for students	75	0.22
Availability and helpfulness	68	0.29
Overall course	92	0.51
Overall instructor	109	0.61
Miscellaneous	47	0.23

students' evaluations of the instructor's interest (dimension 1), only seven are based solely on the instructor's interest; the other thirty-six validity coefficients are based on from two to sixteen other dimensions of instructional effectiveness. Furthermore, there is variability in these results from study to study.

Implications for Personnel Decisions

The results of the uniformity analysis suggest that the items on multidimensional student rating forms, as well as the factors they represent, vary across study findings. Especially at the level of asking specific questions about instruction (that is, low-inference questions; Murray, 1983), student-ratings forms are diverse. Furthermore, even as the items are organized into factors, a considerable lack of uniformity remains. For example, suppose that two instructors are evaluated by their students. Instructor A uses the Michigan State Student Instructional Rating (MSSIR), while instructor B uses the Student Instructional Report (SIR). Both forms include a factor labeled "Course Organization," but in the MSSIR report it taps dimension 5, while in the SIR system it taps dimensions 2 and 8. The two forms are not comparable. Were instructor B to score low on course organization, as compared to instructor A, it would be incorrect to infer that he was less skilled than instructor A in preparing himself for instruction.

Are there clusters of higher-order (that is, high-inference) factors that provide more evidence of uniformity? This was the next phase of our quantitative synthesis. Feldman (1976) identifies three clusters, which he calls Instructor's Presentation of Material, Instructor's Facilitation of Learning, and Instructor's Regulation of Students. We will attempt to determine whether these clusters (or others) are uniform higher-order factors of multidimensional ratings. Unfortunately, such a finding, if correct, would do little to eliminate the uniformity problem in existing multidimensional rating forms, since items are fixed at the lowest level of operation or inference. Therefore, we suggest that evaluations for summative purposes be based on global items; we advise against the use of multidimensional rating forms for summative decisions.

Other Uses

The information provided by multidimensional rating forms has the potential for useful application to purposes other than summative ratings. For example, with the right conditions, and with students' global judgments influenced by factor ratings, factor scores may be useful for understanding how students arrive at global decisions about teaching effectiveness. Once these common, high-inference clusters have been determined, instructors and administrators should consider a modified "cafeteria" approach to the selection of specific items for formative evaluations of teaching.

In typical "cafeteria" approaches to instructional evaluation, a limited selection is made from a large bank of specific items. (The dimensions and examples listed elsewhere in this chapter are a good basis for such an item bank.) Inherent in this approach, however, is an assumption that instructors know the qualities of good teaching—for themselves, their courses, and their students—and that this knowledge is reflected in their selection of items for rating, and that instructors therefore learn whether the delivery of these characteristics needs improvement through the ratings they receive. They do not learn, however, whether the characteristics they have selected are appropriate (that is, items that affect learning) to the situation.

A modified "cafeteria" approach may help instructors learn about the appropriateness of characteristics. Instructors using this approach select specific items, but their selections are influenced by knowledge of the major teaching clusters. The teaching clusters provide some guidance to the teaching characteristics that should be evaluated. Nevertheless, this remains an idiosyncratic approach to formative evaluation. For one thing, it limits the degree to which meaningful comparisons with other instructors and courses can be made.

Alternatively, locally developed and validated rating forms can be used for formative purposes, in place of the standard multi-item form or the item bank. Comparisons across instructors and courses are thereby facilitated, but problems of content validity may result if the forms are not specific to instructional contexts. For example, instructors designing a departmentwide form may not consider distinctions among lecture and discussion formats, methodology and practical content, and so on.

We caution, however, that even these uses of factor scores may be unproductive if students' judgments about teaching are formed primarily on the basis of global assessments that influence impressions of particular teaching factors (a result sometimes referred to as the *halo effect*). In addition, any correlation between factor scores and global ratings may come about through a third variable. For example, an instructor's influence on actual learning and motivation may affect both global and factor ratings.

Finally, we wish to draw attention to the long-standing tradition among faculty (even those who accept the principle of student ratings) to criticize particular items that appear on multi-item forms. Such criticisms are almost as frequent and strong as the complaints that student evaluations are popularity contests and that students cannot judge how well they have learned. Debate and disagreement among faculty over specific rating items should not be ignored. For example, if the goal is to know whether a professor is an outstanding instructor, then ask that question. What need is their to infer this quality from an item on the instructor's friendliness or on the perceived difficulty of the course?

References

Abrami, P. C. "Dimensions of Effective College Instruction." *Review of Higher Education,* 1985, *8,* 211–228.

Abrami, P. C. "SEEQ and Ye Shall Find: A Review of Marsh's 'Students' Evaluation of University Teaching.'" *Instructional Evaluation,* 1988, *9,* 19–27.

Abrami, P. C. "How Should We Use Student Ratings to Evaluate Teaching?" *Research in Higher Education,* 1989a, *30,* 221–227.

Abrami, P. C. "SEEQing the Truth About Student Ratings of Instruction." *Educational Researcher,* 1989b, *43,* 43–45.

Abrami, P. C., Cohen, P. A., and d'Apollonia, S. "Implementation Problems in Meta-Analysis." *Review of Educational Research,* 1988, *58,* 151–179.

Abrami, P. C., d'Apollonia, S., and Cohen, P. A. "The Validity of Student Ratings of Instruction: What We Know and What We Don't." *Journal of Educational Psychology,* 1990, *82,* 219–231.

Abrami, P. C., Leventhal, L., and Perry, R. P. "Educational Seduction." *Review of Educational Research,* 1982, *52,* 446–464.

Cohen, P. A. "Student Ratings of Instruction and Student Achievement: A Meta-Analysis of Multisection Validity Studies." *Review of Educational Research,* 1981, *51,* 281–309.

Feldman, K. A. "The Superior College Teacher from the Student's View." *Research in Higher Education,* 1976, *5,* 243–288.

Feldman, K. A. "Consistency and Variability Among College Students in Rating Their Teachers and Courses." *Research in Higher Education,* 1977, *6,* 223–274.

Feldman, K. A. "Course Characteristics and College Students' Ratings of Their Teachers and Courses: What We Know and What We Don't." *Research in Higher Education,* 1978, *9,* 199–242.

Feldman, K. A. "The Significance of Circumstances for College Students' Ratings of Their Teachers and Courses." *Research in Higher Education,* 1979, *10,* 149–172.

Feldman, K. A. "Seniority and Experience of College Teachers as Related to Evaluations They Receive from Students." *Research in Higher Education,* 1983, *18,* 3–124.

Feldman, K. A. "Class Size and College Students' Evaluations of Teachers and Courses: A Closer Look." *Research in Higher Education,* 1984, *21,* 45–116.

Feldman, K. A. "Instructional Effectiveness of College Teachers as Judged by Teachers Themselves, Current and Former Students, Colleagues, Administrators, and External (Neutral) Observers." *Research in Higher Education,* 1989, *30,* 137–194.

Franklin, J., and Theall, M. "Who Reads Ratings: Knowledge, Attitudes, and Practices of Users of Student Ratings of Instruction." Paper presented at the annual meeting of the American Educational Research Association, San Francisco, 1989.

Marsh, H. W. "Students' Evaluations of University Teaching: Research Findings, Methodological Issues, and Directions for Future Research." *International Journal of Educational Research,* 1987, *11,* 253–388.

Marsh, H. W., and Hocevar, D. "The Factorial Invariance of Student Evaluations of College Teaching." *American Educational Research Journal,* 1984, *21,* 341–366.

Murray, H. G. "Low-Inference Classroom Teaching Behaviors in Relation to Six Measures of College Teaching Effectiveness." Paper presented at the Conference on the Evaluation and Improvement of University Teaching, Montebello, Quebec, 1983.

Philip C. Abrami is director of the Centre for the Study of Classroom Processes and professor of education at Concordia University, Montreal.

Sylvia d'Apollonia is a member of the Centre for the Study of Classroom Processes, Concordia University, and professor of biology at Vanier College, Montreal.

Research on the variables that may bias student ratings has largely found these variables to have little influence. One exception concerns academic fields. Institutions and individuals should decide how they will take academic-field differences into consideration when they interpret student ratings.

Students Do Rate Different Academic Fields Differently

William E. Cashin

If you ask a college teacher whether students rate different academic fields differently, he or she will most probably say yes. If you ask why, you are not likely to be given much justification beyond the conviction that different fields are different. Nevertheless, there is increasing evidence that the conventional wisdom is correct. Students do rate academic fields differently. What is not clear is why.

Feldman (1978), in the fourth of his series of comprehensive reviews of various aspects of the student-ratings literature, examines the relationships of a variety of course characteristics to student ratings. He reviewed eleven studies (seven were of single institutions) that presented data on the ratings of different academic fields. He ranked the different fields and then compared the standardized ranks. He concluded that English, the humanities, the arts, and foreign languages tend to fall into the high and medium rankings. The social sciences (especially political science, sociology, psychology, and economics) tend to fall into the medium or low rankings. Science fields (except certain areas of the biological sciences), mathematics, and engineering tend to fall into the lower rankings.

Since then, there have been relatively few studies of how students rate different academic fields, and those published tend to be within single institutions and often within specific colleges of universities (for example, Cranton and Smith, 1986, studied only business courses). Nevertheless, comparative data for different academic fields have been published for two widely used student rating systems: the Student Instructional Report (SIR), from the Educational Testing Service, and the Instructional Development and Effectiveness Assessment (IDEA) system, from Kansas State University.

NEW DIRECTIONS FOR TEACHING AND LEARNING, no. 43, Fall 1990 © Jossey-Bass Inc., Publishers

Both sets of data, as well as all the studies reviewed by Feldman (1978), are user samples, or so-called norms of convenience—that is, the data represent only the institutions that chose to use the two systems. Neither the Educational Testing Service nor Kansas State University's Center for Faculty Evaluation and Development suggest that their data bases constitute normative data for higher education in general; both speak of comparative data. Nevertheless, SIR and IDEA are probably the two most widely used student rating systems in North America. Their comparative data probably constitute the broadest sample of academic-field data now available. Examination of these two data bases should provide useful information about the ways in which students generally rate different academic fields.

Student Instructional Report (SIR)

Educational Testing Service (ETS) has published SIR comparative guides for four-year institutions (Educational Testing Service, 1979 and 1982a) and two-year institutions (Educational Testing Service, 1977 and 1982b). ETS plans to publish its third set of comparative data guides in 1990. The 1977 comparative guide for two-year institutions reports data from 5,960 classes for thirty-one academic fields or combinations of fields. The 1979 comparative guide for four-year institutions also reports data for thirty-one fields (not necessarily identical to the fields in the two-year guide) from 8,181 classes. The more recent comparative guides report data for twenty-three fields for two-year institutions, from 7,418 classes, and for twenty-seven fields for four-year institutions, from 4,954 classes. These guides present data for all thirty-nine of the SIR items. The SIR item used to measure course effectiveness was "I would rate the overall value of this course to me as (5) Excellent, (4) Good, (3) Above Average, (2) Fair, (1) Poor." SIR reports data from two different items measuring instructor effectiveness, both using a 5-point scale. In the 1970s, the item read as follows: "Compared to other instructors you have had (secondary school and college), how effective has the instructor been in this course?" For the 1982 data, SIR used a new item: "How would you rate the quality of instruction in this course?"

Instructional Development and Effectiveness Assessment (IDEA)

Comparative data for various academic fields have also been reported in two IDEA technical reports. Data for all thirty-nine IDEA items were reported for nine groupings of academic fields (Cashin and Slawson, 1977). More recently (Cashin, Noma, and Hanna, 1987), IDEA data have been reported for forty-four different academic fields from 87,843 classes for 316 colleges and universities (two- and four-year institutions combined; 24

percent were two-year institutions). Unlike SIR, which uses a new sample of data each time, the IDEA data were aggregated from 1975 (when IDEA was first made available to colleges and universities other than Kansas State University, where the system was developed) to 1985. Moreover, the 1987 IDEA technical report (Cashin, Noma, and Hanna, 1987) presented data for only three global measures: (1) "I would like to take another course from this instructor"; (2) "As a result of taking this course, I have more positive feelings toward this field of study"; and (3) a composite measure, related to the extent to which students report having made progress on the objectives selected for specific courses. Objective-related items concern such things as gaining factual knowledge, developing oral or writing skills, and developing a sense of personal responsibility. Data presented for these three global items also take into consideration the students' motivation level (their desire to take the course) and the size of the class.

Summarizing the Data

Examining the actual means for the SIR and IDEA data would be informative, but Table 1 attempts to present the results more simply. Following the procedure used by Feldman (1978), the fields for each data set were divided into three groups: high, medium, and low. The groupings were rather rough because the number of fields in each set was not always divisible by three, and because there were ties in the ratings of some fields at the division point. In such cases, fields were put into either the high or the low group, rather than into the medium group. As a result, proportionately fewer fields were classified as medium. The IDEA data were counted twice because of the larger size of the data base that was used. Each academic field was then examined, to determine how often it fell into the high, medium, or low group. There was a possible maximum of six data sets: IDEA (counted twice), two SIR-4 sets, and two SIR-2 sets. For most fields, however, there were only three or four sets; for four fields, there were only IDEA data.

The academic fields listed in the high group fell into that group for all the sets that had data for that field. Similarly, the fields listed in the low group (and, to a certain extent, those in the medium group) were in those groups for all data sets. (There were three exceptions in the medium group under "Instructor Effectiveness"; see the note in Table 1.) The medium-high group tended to receive medium and high rankings; the medium-low group tended to receive medium and low rankings. The fields in all five groups are listed alphabetically. No attempt has been made to differentiate among fields within a group; to do so would probably risk overinterpretation of the data (that is, suggestion of differences unwarranted by the precision of the data).

Looking just at "Course Effectiveness," we see that the results are

Table 1. Summary of Ratings on Course Effectiveness and Instructor Effectiveness for IDEA and SIR Academic-Field Data

Field	Item Measure	
	Course Effectiveness	*Instructor Effectiveness*

High

Architecture	Area studies
Art	Fine and applied arts
Communications	Foreign languages
Fine and applied arts	Military sciences
Health and technology	Music
Home economics	
Music	
Secretarial studies	
Speech	

Medium-High

Agriculture	Art
Education	Communications
Foreign languages	English language and literature
Letters and humanities	Health and technology
Library science	History
Nursing	Home economics
Physical and health education	Law
Political science and government	Letters and humanities
Public affairs	Library science
Religion and theology	Physical and health education
Social work and service	Political science and government
Trade and vocational-technical	Psychology
education	Public affairs
	Religion and theology
	Secretarial studies
	Speech
	Trade and vocational-technical
	education

Medium

Area studies	Business and commercial technology[a]
Biological sciences	Education[a]
Health professions	Engineering technology
Interdisciplinary studies	Nursing[a]
Military sciences	
Psychology	

Medium-Low

Accounting	Agriculture
Business and commercial technology	Biological sciences
English language and literature	Chemistry
History	Health professions
Law	Mathematics and statistics
Social sciences	Philosophy

Table 1. (*continued*)

Field	Course Effectiveness	Instructor Effectiveness
		Item Measure
	Sociology	Social sciences
		Social work and service
		Sociology

Low

Business and management	Accounting
Chemistry	Architecture
Computer and information science	Business and management
Data-processing technology	Computer and information science
Economics	Data-processing technology
Engineering	Economics
Engineering technology	Engineering
Mathematics and statistics	Interdisciplinary studies
Philosophy	Physical sciences
Physical sciences	Physics
Physics	

[a] These fields received mixed rankings but would average 2 if high = 3, medium = 2, and low = 1.

similar to Feldman's (1978) conclusions. The high group tends to consist of the arts and humanities. This trend is not universal, however; English language and literature and history both fall into the medium-low group. The low group tends to consist mostly of business, economics, computer science, math, physical sciences, and engineering. The biological and social sciences and health and other professions tend to fall somewhere in the middle.

If we look at "Course Effectiveness" and "Instructor Effectiveness" combined, we see that fine and applied arts and music fall into the high group for both measures. If we consider fields that are high on one measure but medium-high on the other, art, communications, foreign languages and literatures, home economics, secretarial studies, and speech also fall toward the high end. This is very much a humanities cluster, with the exception of home economics and secretarial studies.

Several fields fall into the low group for both course effectiveness and instructor effectiveness: business and management, computer and information sciences, data-processing technologies, economics, engineering, physical sciences, and physics. To the fields that were low on one measure and medium-low on the other we must add accounting, chemistry, mathematical sciences, and philosophy. This is very much a math-science-technical cluster, with the exception of philosophy and, perhaps, business and management.

Implications for Decision Makers

The primary implication (if we are convinced by the foregoing data that different academic fields are rated differently) is that we need to decide what to do about this phenomenon when we interpret student-ratings data. Administrators can no longer look at data from a variety of fields and unquestioningly compare numbers directly. Instructors cannot look at two courses they are teaching and necessarily assume, if their ratings for the two courses are the same, that they taught both courses equally well.

The real problem arises from our not knowing why the different fields are rated differently. This finding is not due just to variations in students' motivation (for example, required versus elective courses) or class size. In one unpublished analysis of IDEA data it was found, even after the researchers controlled for students' motivation and class size, that differences in academic fields explained an additional 10 percent or more of the variance for some IDEA course objectives. In another study of a sample of IDEA data (Cashin and Clegg, 1987), 14 to 58 percent of the remaining variance was explained after controlling for differences among institutions, in number of courses for each field, in students' motivation, and in class size.

There are several possible explanations for differences in the ratings of different academic fields. One is that the more quantitative courses tend to receive lower ratings. The low fields tend to be math, science, engineering, and quantitative business course (for example, accounting and economics). A possible explanation for these differences is that students' quantitative skills are more poorly developed than their verbal skills. This would make quantitative courses more difficult to teach. Moreover, quantitative courses may receive lower ratings because students have lower expectations of success and lower actual rates of success. We have evidence that higher student ratings are related to students' achievement and satisfaction (Cohen, 1981) and that, as grades decrease, students more frequently attribute their poor performance to factors external to themselves (Theall, Franklin, and Ludlow, 1990). Students' dissatisfaction with poor performance may be reflected in lower ratings.

Another explanation of different ratings for different fields is that the more sequential courses, where success depends heavily on the mastery of material from a previous course, tend to receive lower ratings. This holds true for most math and science courses and for many professional courses, but it also holds true for foreign-language courses, which tend not to receive low ratings. Sequential courses may receive lower ratings because today's students are not studying as much as students have in previous decades and so do not have as solid a foundation for the courses that come later in a sequence.

Still another explanation involves how specifiable and masterable the course content is. There is probably much more agreement on the course content for Calculus I or Physics I than there is for Psychology I or American History I. If one were to draw a circle to include the possible content for Calculus I and for History I, the circle for Calculus I would be much smaller, and this implies that the content would be more masterable. To the extent that this explanation is true, it presents a paradox, for students tend to give lower ratings to fields where the course content is more clearly defined, less extensive, and probably more masterable. Perhaps the clearer the students are about what they are to learn, the more aware they are of the limitations of their learning. Again, this may be because students do not study as much as they did in previous decades, but it may also be because students operate from the erroneous assumption that they should learn 80 to 100 percent of the course material. The potential content domain of most college courses is so vast that it cannot even be defined. Obviously, then, such content can never be mastered. An alternative explanation would be that the less specifiable courses allow for more creativity, and that there are more possible "correct answers." Thus, there would be greater freedom and possibly higher performance, and so higher ratings.

Yet another explanation is that students in different majors rate courses differently, because of differences in attitude, in academic skills and goals, in motivation, in learning styles, or in models of effective teaching. Although students majoring in any given field are likely to vary in many ways, it is quite possible that, taken as a group, they have certain characteristics that are related to how they rate courses and instructors.

Another explanation concerns the function of the course in the curriculum (for example, the course may be used to screen out weak students). Such courses may deliberately be made difficult and do not emphasize helping students learn. Students would understandably tend to give such courses lower ratings.

A final explanation may be that some academic fields are poorly taught. Many of the low-rated fields are those in which institutions must pay very high salaries even to compete modestly with business and industry. Perhaps the faculty teaching those courses are less effective as a group than faculty in some other fields. It costs far less to hire an outstanding teacher in English than it does to hire an outstanding teacher in computer science, accounting, or engineering. It costs far less to hire an outstanding teacher in English than it does to hire an outstanding teacher in computer science, accounting, or engineering.

Probably the real explanation lies in some combination of the explanations just offered. Few studies discuss more than one of these explanations, and often the studies are contradictory. Until research can provide more definite data to explain the relationships between background variables and student ratings of different academic fields, faculty and administrators will have to create their own hypotheses and collect their own data.

My suggestion is that each institution gather student-ratings data on its own academic fields. If an institutionwide form is used, it will be fairly straightforward, but if the institution is using a variety of rating forms, as many institutions do, then some common questions should be developed to permit comparisons across fields on the common items. For such comparisons, I suggest global items dealing with the teaching effectiveness of the instructor, the educational value of the course, and how much students have learned.

Having gathered comparison data for the various academic fields in the institution, one should check to see whether students actually do rate different fields differently. (If there are differences, it would also be interesting to check how these compare with the research summarized in this chapter.) Second, assuming that there are differences, some judgment must be made about the extent to which they reflect differences in the teaching effectiveness of the different departments. Making this judgment will be the most difficult and probably the most controversial part of the task.

At most institutions, there probably already exists a shared perception (or misperception) of teaching effectiveness in many programs. Moreover, each institution typically has data that would provide some basis for this (mis)perception. The students' entrance credentials and, often, data from placement tests are available. Many fields compile scores on licensing and certification exams or scores from the various tests that students take to get into graduate school, and there are usually impressions about how students from different disciplines have performed in the world of work or in subsequent academic programs.

If the institution decides that the differences in student ratings are essentially due to differences in teaching effectiveness (that is, if teaching is poorer in a given department), then these differences should not be statistically adjusted. I think it likely that most institutions will decide that academic-field differences do not provide the complete explanation. If this is the case, then institutions must decide what to do about the differences in student ratings on their campuses. Fairness to faculty and students requires no less.

References

Cashin, W. E., and Clegg, V. L. "Are Student Ratings of Different Academic Fields Different?" Paper presented at the annual meeting of the American Educational Research Association, Chicago, 1987.

Cashin, W. E., Noma, A., and Hanna, G. S. *IDEA Technical Report No. 6: Comparative Data by Academic Field.* Manhattan: Center for Faculty Evaluation and Development, Kansas State University, 1987.

Cashin, W. E., and Slawson, H. M. *IDEA Technical Report No. 3: Description of Data Base, 1977–78.* Manhattan: Center for Faculty Evaluation and Development, Kansas State University, 1977.

Cohen, P. A. "Student Ratings of Instruction and Student Achievement: A Meta-Analysis of Multisection Validity Studies." *Review of Educational Research*, 1981, *51*, 281–309.

Cranton, P. A., and Smith, R. A. "A New Look at the Effect of Course Characteristics on Student Ratings of Instruction." *American Educational Research Journal,* 1986, 23, 117-128.

Educational Testing Service. *Student Instructional Report: Comparative Data Guide for Two-Year Colleges and Technical Institutions.* Princeton, N.J.: Educational Testing Service, 1977.

Educational Testing Service. *Student Instructional Report: Comparative Data Guide for Four-Year Colleges and Universities.* Princeton, N.J.: Educational Testing Service, 1979.

Educational Testing Service. *Student Instructional Report: Comparative Data Guide for Four-Year Colleges and Universities.* Princeton, N.J.: Educational Testing Service, 1982a.

Educational Testing Service. *Student Instructional Report: Comparative Data Guide for Two-Year Colleges and Technical Institutions.* Princeton, N.J.: Educational Testing Service, 1982b.

Feldman, K. A. "Course Characteristics and College Students' Ratings of Their Teachers and Courses: What We Know and What We Don't." *Research in Higher Education,* 1978, 9, 199-242.

Theall, M., Franklin, J., and Ludlow, L. H. "Attributions and Retributions: Student Ratings and the Perceived Causes of Performance." Paper presented at the annual meeting of the American Educational Research Association, Boston, 1990.

William E. Cashin is director of the Center for Faculty Evaluation and Development, Division of Continuing Education, Kansas State University.

Student ratings have been studied exhaustively. Why has the research not found its way into everyday practice?

Bringing Research into Practice

Peter A. Cohen

Student ratings have been studied to death. We have created a voluminous literature on the reliability, validity, potential biases, and conditions for use of student ratings, and yet this body of knowledge has not been completely translated into practice. In fact, relevant research is largely ignored in practice. In this chapter, I will discuss, from my perspective as a researcher and practitioner in instructional evaluation, why research has had such a limited impact on practice and how future research can be focused, to lead to improved use of student ratings.

More than any other effort to date, Franklin and Theall's (1989) work highlights what faculty and administrators actually know about the student-ratings literature and how their knowledge compares with that of experts. In one sense, it is encouraging to note the degree of expert consensus in this area. Although controversy surrounding student ratings has existed for years, experts draw consistent, sound conclusions that are based on this literature. I find the lack of knowledge displayed by the consumers of this research—faculty and administrators—distressing. The potential danger here, of course, lies in the misuse of information in decisions on tenure and promotion made by administrators who are unaware of critical variables and conditions affecting the interpretation of student ratings.

Myths

My experience with the consumers of student ratings reflects Franklin and Theall's (1989) findings about the relationship between attitudes and knowledge—that is, faculty and administrators who have negative attitudes toward student ratings seem not to know what the research tells us about ratings. Experts may agree on student-ratings issues, but faculty hold many misconceptions about the literature. When working with different groups of faculty and administrators, I refer to these misconceptions as *myths*. The seven myths I have most frequently encountered are listed here:

1. Students are not qualified to make judgments about teaching competence.
2. Student ratings are popularity contests.
3. Students are not able to make accurate judgments until after they have been away from the course for several years.
4. Student ratings are unreliable.
5. Student ratings are invalid.
6. Students rate instructors on the basis of the grades they receive.
7. Extraneous variables and conditions affect student ratings.

All of these concerns have been addressed extensively in the research literature (see, for example, reviews by Braskamp, Brandenburg, and Ory, 1984; Marsh, 1987). We can attempt to dispel these myths with research-based refutations:

1. Students are qualified to rate certain dimensions of teaching.
2. Students do discriminate among dimensions of teaching and do not judge solely on the popularity of instructors.
3. Ratings by current students are highly correlated with those of former students (alumni).
4. Student ratings are reliable in terms of both *agreement* (similarity among students rating a course and the instructor) and *stability* (the extent to which the same student rates the course and the instructor similarly at two different times).
5. Student ratings are valid, as measured against a number of criteria, particularly students' learning.
6. Student ratings are not unduly influenced by the grades students receive or expect to receive.
7. Student ratings are not unduly affected by such external factors as student characteristics, course characteristics, and teacher characteristics.

Our challenge, as action-oriented researchers, is to convince administrators to follow sound ratings practice that is based on research. At one level, we can attempt to make faculty and administrators more receptive to ratings by increasing their awareness of the research in this area, but simply disseminating research findings does not move faculty and administrators to action. Negative attitudes toward student ratings are especially resistant to change, and it seems that faculty and administrators support their belief in student-ratings myths with personal and anecdotal evidence, which outweighs empirically based research evidence. We invest enormous energy in counteracting these myths, with relatively little effect.

What can be particularly damaging to the acceptance of student ratings is that, in some settings and in certain conditions, a myth may have some basis in fact. Let me provide an example involving extraneous factors that may affect student ratings (myth 7). Contrary to common belief, workload and course difficulty are not strongly related to course ratings, and the small relationship that does exist is in the opposite direction of what might be expected—that is, students tend to rate difficult, high-workload courses higher than less difficult, low-workload courses (Marsh, 1987). Therefore, the notion that students downgrade courses that are difficult can be considered a myth.

We have found, however, that course workload did function as a potential biasing factor of student ratings in a dental school. In this environment, high-workload courses were rated significantly lower than low-workload courses (Cohen and Benson, 1988). When a course-rating system was first implemented at this school, faculty believed that student ratings were biased according to workload of courses. In this case, they were right. Gaining faculty acceptance for the student-ratings system proved difficult and was possible only after this potential biasing factor was accounted for by separate reporting of student-ratings norms for courses categorized as having high and low workloads. As advocates of student ratings, we need to distinguish between those negative attitudes based on reality and those based on myth and act accordingly.

Conflict and Controversy

With thousands of published studies on various aspects of student ratings, we should be able to derive meaningful findings that can be applied to evaluation practice. I have implied that nonsupportive attitudes among faculty and administrators may be one potential barrier, but I think a more serious one has been the conflicting findings and arguments about student ratings presented by researchers and reviewers.

Let us look at student-ratings validity research. Systematic research on students' ratings of instruction was initiated in the late 1920s by Remmers and his associates, who focused on reliability, validity, and bias issues. Later, this group conducted the first multisection validity study of student ratings, in which students were assigned to different sections of the same course, and section-average achievement was correlated with section-average student ratings (Remmers, Martin, and Elliott, 1949). Studies using this paradigm reached a peak in the 1970s and spawned tremendous controversy and debate. It became difficult to draw firm conclusions about the validity of student ratings. Supporters and detractors took their stands, selectively citing studies to support their arguments. These debates were reflected in reviews of this research. A prime example was the use of the controversial Rodin and Rodin (1972) article, which showed a strong negative correlation between ratings and learning and was used primarily to argue against the use of student ratings. For a time during the height of the controversy, this was the most often cited study on student ratings (Cohen, 1983). Several reviewers have since impugned the design and interpretation of the Rodin and Rodin study, but for many years it weakened faith in the validity of student ratings. Trends in citing this study over the past two decades are shown in Figure 1. There was a substantial number of citations from 1973 to 1980, but there was a significant drop in the citation rate after 1980. I believe that the lowered citation rate of this study reflects moderation in the general debate over student-ratings validity. During the past decade, the quieting of this controversy has been due in no small part to the advent of new methodologies for reviewing and synthesizing the research literature.

Meta-Analysis and the Student-Ratings Literature

The increasing use of techniques for quantitative research synthesis has allowed us to make sense out of conflicting research findings. Glass (1976) coined the term *meta-analysis,* and a new era for depicting, organizing, and interpreting study findings began. He defined this method formally as

Figure 1. Rodin and Rodin Citations, by Year

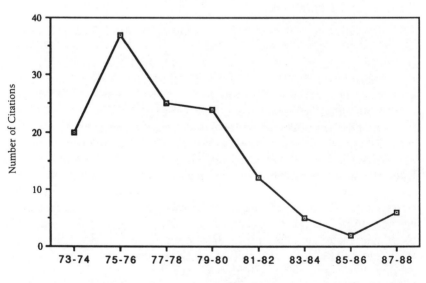

Year

statistical analysis of a large collection of results from individual studies, for the purpose of integrating findings. The reviewer who conducts a meta-analysis first specifies criteria for including studies in the analysis and then locates studies through clearly specified search procedures. The meta-analysis codes the features of studies and calculates individual study outcomes. Finally, he or she uses multivariate techniques and advanced statistical methods to describe findings and relate features of the studies to outcomes.

The problems of relying on meta-analysis as a cure-all for controversies have been addressed by Abrami, Cohen, and d'Apollonia (1988) and by Slavin (1984). Over the past ten years, however, meta-analysis has demonstrated several actual and potential advantages over traditional narrative reviews of the literature. Five of these advantages illustrate how this modern method has contributed to better understanding of student ratings. Since its application to the student-ratings literature, beginning in 1980, meta-analysis has (1) provided general conclusions about the student-ratings literature, (2) related study outcomes to study features, (3) highlighted areas that have been studied in depth and those in need of further study, (4) determined standards for empirical research studies, and (5) elevated the quality of student-ratings literature reviews.

How has meta-analysis enhanced understanding of the student-ratings literature? Given the almost incredibly vast literature, which consists of conflicting findings and multiple interpretations, traditional narrative reviewers of the student-ratings literature failed to collect studies systematically and effectively synthesize their results. Recent meta-analyses, by contrast, have offered sound general conclusions about student ratings. For example, on the basis of the literature on multisection validity, we can say that overall course and instructor ratings, as well as a number of more specific dimensions of teaching, are related to students' achievement (Cohen, 1981, 1986; d'Apollonia and Abrami, 1988). We also have learned that student-ratings feedback by itself contributes only modestly to instructional improvement. When used in conjunction with a consultant, however, it leads to greater improvement (Cohen, 1980; L'Hommedieu, Menges, and Brinko, 1988). In laboratory studies of the influence that instructors' enthusiasm has on ratings, instructors' expressiveness has been shown to have a substantial impact on ratings but only a small impact on achievement, while lecture content has been shown to have a substantial impact on achievement but only a small impact on ratings (Abrami, Leventhal, and Perry, 1982). We also know that faculty and students generally value various aspects of teaching similarly (Feldman, 1988). Meta-analyses such as these disclose findings that are not evident in other reviews of the student-ratings literature.

Meta-analysis offers a second, potential advantage over traditional narrative reviews by allowing us to relate study features to study outcomes.

There are many complexities involved in student-ratings research, such as those that concern the use of the appropriate unit of analysis, the multidimensional nature of ratings, the conditions in which ratings are administered, and the variety of settings in which studies are conducted. A study-feature analysis helps us determine whether differences in outcomes are related to potential biasing factors in study design or whether outcomes vary as a result of study conditions. A few student-ratings meta-analyses have uncovered simple relationships between some study features and study outcomes (Cohen, 1981; L'Hommedieu, Menges, and Brinko, 1988), but the potential of relating study characteristics to study outcomes in the student-ratings literature has yet to be fully realized. To aid practitioners, future meta-analytic efforts will need not only to identify true explanatory characteristics but also to distinguish, on the one hand, the degree of their generalizability across settings and, on the other, the degree to which particular relationships exist in particular conditions (Abrami, d'Apollonia, and Cohen, 1990).

A third advantage of meta-analysis over traditional narrative review is its ability to capture the representativeness of the student-ratings literature. From meta-analyses we can determine which areas need further study. Considering the literature on multisection validity, for example, Abrami and his colleagues (Abrami, Cohen, and d'Apollonia, 1988; Abrami, d'Apollonia, and Cohen, 1990) identified forty-three studies and seventy-five possible study characteristics. They concluded that prior reviews and meta-analyses had not adequately identified potential study features, and that future reviewers should systematically examine the characteristics investigated, accounted for, and mentioned in a set of studies.

A fourth advantage of meta-analysis is that it provides standards for further empirical research on student ratings. For example, investigators have outlined, in some detail, criteria for conducting high-quality research in such areas as student-ratings feedback (L'Hommedieu, Menges, and Brinko, 1990), student-ratings validity, using the multisection-validity paradigm (Abrami, d'Apollonia, and Cohen, 1990; Cohen, 1983), and even meta-analysis (Abrami, Cohen, and d'Apollonia, 1988). Because of the standards set by meta-analysis, many journals now require empirical research to report results in formats that can be incorporated into a quantitative review, thus encouraging future studies to provide results in a similarly interpretable fashion.

The fifth advantage of meta-analysis is that it has effectively raised our expectations regarding the quality of the literature reviews concerning student ratings. Pre-1980 reviews tended to be selective and allowed for reviewer bias. With an emphasis on replicability of methods, meta-analysis has encouraged even narrative reviewers to be more systematic. Consequently, we have some excellent narrative reviews of the overall student-ratings literature (Cashin, 1988; Marsh, 1987) and of recommendations for use (Cashin, 1990), as well as of more specific issues concerning student ratings (Feldman, 1983, 1984, 1986).

Over the past decade, the evolution of better methods, both quantitative and qualitative, for reviewing the literature have helped us improve our organization and interpretation of study findings. Because of these efforts, researchers are in much greater agreement about the reliability, validity, and use of student ratings. We are now at a point where these general conclusions must be translated into practice.

Reducing Resistance to Student Ratings

We should not attempt to educate all faculty and administrators on the intricacies of student ratings; rather, we should intensify our efforts to train those who offer their services to faculty and administrators. According to the evidence provided by Franklin and Theall (1989), decision makers simply are not very knowledgeable about student ratings, and yet they regularly use these data in making decisions about promotion and tenure. It is unreasonable to expect faculty and administrators, of their own accord, to become familiar enough with the evaluation literature to make sound judgments concerning the use of student ratings. It is more appropriate for key resource people—primarily specialists in instructional development and evaluation—to serve as local experts, summarizing research findings for faculty and administrators and facilitating proper student-ratings practice.

Nevertheless, the problem still remains of having decision makers accept the results of ratings research. Instructional resource people may help disseminate research findings and conclusions on student ratings, but they may not be able to convince decision makers to use results appropriately. Telling faculty and administrators how a student-ratings system should work is rarely effective. In fact, a major source of resistance to the implementation of evaluation systems is the lack of faculty's and administrators' input into the development of those systems (Cohen, 1988).

To minimize resistance to evaluation systems is as crucial as to disseminate knowledge about the research, perhaps even more crucial when the purpose is to affect behavioral change. In general, people resist change, and implementing or revising a student-ratings system involves change for faculty and administrators. I have found that attitudes and beliefs about a specific evaluation system are often better predictors of its acceptance than is knowledge of the evaluation literature. Some years ago, I participated in a project designed to reduce resistance to the introduction of a state-of-the-art sonar system on U.S. Navy destroyers (Abrams, Sheposh, Cohen, and Young, 1977). The problem we encountered then is analogous to the poor student-ratings practice we are faced with today. Many sonar operators did not use the various functions and features of the new sonar system properly, even though they had received formal training. To facilitate acceptance of the new system, we gave operators positive experiences and opportunities to evaluate the system realistically, limitations included. Further, we found that designating an influential "change advocate" on board the ships facilitated the acceptance of the new system. The change advocate encouraged participation in exercises, provided information on causes of system misuse, and helped operators diagnose the causes of any misuse that did occur.

Instructional resource people in our institutions can also target change advocates—namely, faculty or administrators—who will realize and speak for the importance of improved evaluation and development services. These advocates must be viewed as credible voices within the existing system. To the extent that student-ratings systems are implemented in appropriate conditions and faculty have input into the systems, there will be more positive experiences. Although faculty attitudes may improve with time and experience, even a good system may need to be renewed every seven to ten years because of such factors as the system's inflexibility, disagreements over wording of items, and potential sources of bias (Ory and Brandenburg, 1985).

Bringing Research into Practice

Many faculty and administrators harbor misconceptions about student ratings, and these affect interpretations and uses of ratings. Rather than clarifying these misconceptions, conflicting research results have fueled controversy in this area. During the past decade, however, the advent of methods for quantitative review have made it possible to draw firm conclusions from the student-ratings literature. Although this potential exists, we have yet to successfully communicate these findings to decision makers in ways that can get our knowledge translated into effective practice.

I would like to see future research efforts focus on conditions and settings affecting the practice of using student ratings. If we are going to understand why the knowledge we have accumulated is not being used, we will need to explore faculty attitudes toward student ratings. For example, what factors contribute to faculty's misconceptions about student ratings of instruction? How does increased knowledge affect attitudes? Why are some faculty and administrators so critical of student ratings and so resistant to the implementation of student-ratings systems? We should encourage resource people (whether they are faculty members working within departments or instructional developers and evaluators working on a schoolwide basis) to be change advocates, and we should conduct research to determine the effectiveness of this approach. Are attitudes toward student-ratings systems more positive when change advocates are used? Does this approach reduce faulty interpretations and misuse of student ratings on the part of administrators?

Throughout our sixty-year research history, we have learned a great deal about student ratings. We know that they can be a valuable source of information on teaching effectiveness. We understand very little, however, about the actual practice of using such ratings. To fully realize the potential of student ratings, we must uncover the sources of resistance that prevent this valuable source of data from being properly and effectively used.

References

Abrami, P. C., Cohen, P. A., and d'Apollonia, S. "Implementation Problems in Meta-Analysis." *Review of Educational Research*, 1988, *58*, 151–179.

Abrami, P. C., d'Apollonia, S., and Cohen, P. A. "The Literature on the Validity of Student Ratings: What We Know and What We Don't." *Journal of Educational Psychology*, 1990, *82*, 219–231.

Abrami, P. C., Leventhal, L., and Perry, R. P. "Educational Seduction." *Review of Educational Research*, 1982, *52*, 446–464.

Abrams, M. L., Sheposh, J. P., Cohen, P. A., and Young, L. E. *Sonar Operators' Attitudes and Beliefs: Effects on Introduction of New Systems.* San Diego, Calif.: Navy Personnel Research and Development Center, 1977.

Braskamp, L. A., Brandenburg, D. C., and Ory, J. C. *Evaluating Teaching Effectiveness: A Practical Guide.* Newbury Park, Calif.: Sage, 1984.

Cashin, W. E. *Student Ratings of Teaching: A Summary of the Research.* Manhattan: Center for Faculty Evaluation and Development, Kansas State University, 1988.

Cashin, W. E. *Student Ratings of Teaching: Recommendations for Use.* Manhattan: Center for Faculty Evaluation and Development, Kansas State University, 1990.

Cohen, P. A. "Effectiveness of Student-Rating Feedback for Improving College Instruction: A Meta-Analysis of Findings." *Research in Higher Education*, 1980, *13*, 321–341.

Cohen, P. A. "Student Ratings of Instruction and Student Achievement: A Meta-Analysis of Multisection Validity Studies." *Review of Educational Research*, 1981, *51*, 281–309.

Cohen, P. A. "Comment on 'A Selective Review of the Validity of Student Ratings of Teaching.'" *Journal of Higher Education*, 1983, *54*, 448–458.

Cohen, P. A. "An Updated and Expanded Meta-Analysis of Multisection Student Rating Validity Studies." Paper presented at the annual meeting of the American Educational Research Association, San Francisco, 1986.

Cohen, P. A. *Evaluating Teaching Effectiveness.* Washington, D.C.: American Association of Dental Schools, National Curriculum for Dental Faculty Development, 1988.

Cohen, P. A., and Benson, B. A. "Workload and Student Course Ratings in Dental School." *Journal of Dental Education*, 1988, *52*, 98–101.

d'Apollonia, S., and Abrami, P. C. "The Literature on Student Ratings of Instruction: Yet Another Meta-Analysis." Paper presented at the annual meeting of the American Educational Research Association, New Orleans, 1988.

Feldman, K. A. "Seniority and Experience of College Teachers as Related to Evaluations They Receive from Students." *Research in Higher Education*, 1983, *18*, 3–124.

Feldman, K. A. "Class Size and College Students' Evaluations of Teachers and Courses: A Closer Look." *Research in Higher Education*, 1984, *21*, 45–116.

Feldman, K. A. "The Perceived Instructional Effectiveness of College Teachers as Related to Their Personality and Attitudinal Characteristics: A Review and Synthesis." *Research in Higher Education*, 1986, *24*, 139–213.

Feldman, K. A. "Effective College Teaching from the Students' and Faculty's View: Matched or Mismatched Priorities?" *Research in Higher Education*, 1988, 28, 291–344.

Franklin, J., and Theall, M. "Who Reads Ratings: Knowledge, Attitudes, and Practices of Users of Student Ratings of Instruction." Paper presented at the annual meeting of the American Educational Research Association, San Francisco, 1989.

Glass, G. V. "Primary, Secondary, and Meta-Analysis of Research." *Educational Researcher*, 1976, 5, 3–8.

L'Hommedieu, R., Menges, R. J., and Brinko, K. T. *The Effects of Student Ratings Feedback to College Teachers: A Meta-Analysis and Review of Research*. Evanston, Ill.: Center for the Teaching Professions, Northwestern University, 1988.

L'Hommedieu, R., Menges, R. J., and Brinko, K. T. "Methodological Explanations for the Modest Effects of Feedback from Student Ratings." *Journal of Educational Psychology*, 1990, 82, 232–241.

Marsh, H. W. "Students' Evaluations of University Teaching: Research Findings, Methodological Issues, and Directions for Future Research." *International Journal of Educational Research*, 1987, 11, 253–388.

Ory, J. C., and Brandenburg, D. C. "Maintaining a Campus Student Rating System: A Seven-Year Itch." Paper presented at the annual meeting of the American Educational Research Association, Chicago, 1985.

Remmers, H. H., Martin, F. D., and Elliott, D. N. "Are Students' Ratings of Instructors Related to Their Grades?" *Purdue University Studies in Higher Education*, 1949, 66, 17–26.

Rodin, M., and Rodin, B. "Student Evaluations of Teachers." *Science*, 1972, 177, 1164–1166.

Slavin, R. E. "Meta-Analysis in Education: How Has It Been Used?" *Educational Researcher*, 1984, 13, 6–15, 24–27.

Peter A. Cohen is associate professor and director of educational development at the Medical College of Georgia.

INDEX

ORDERING INFORMATION

NEW DIRECTIONS FOR TEACHING AND LEARNING is a series of paperback books that presents ideas and techniques for improving college teaching, based both on the practical expertise of seasoned instructors and on the latest research findings of educational and psychological researchers. Books in the series are published quarterly in Fall, Winter, Spring, and Summer and are available for purchase by subscription as well as by single copy.

SUBSCRIPTIONS for 1990 cost $39.00 for individuals (a savings of 20 percent over single-copy prices) and $52.00 for institutions, agencies, and libraries. Please do not send institutional checks for personal subscriptions. Standing orders are accepted.

SINGLE COPIES cost $12.95 when payment accompanies order. (California, New Jersey, New York, and Washington, D.C., residents please include appropriate sales tax.) Billed orders will be charged postage and handling.

DISCOUNTS FOR QUANTITY ORDERS are available. Please write to the address below for information.

ALL ORDERS must include either the name of an individual or an official purchase order number. Please submit your order as follows:
Subscriptions: specify series and year subscription is to begin
Single copies: include individual title code (such as TL1)

MAIL ALL ORDERS TO:
Jossey-Bass Inc., Publishers
350 Sansome Street
San Francisco, California 94104

This issue of *New Directions for Teaching and Learning* is concerned with collecting, reporting, interpreting, and using student-ratings results—that is, the practice of student ratings. We intend to provide useful information for faculty, administrators, and teaching-improvement practitioners, who make decisions at least partly on the basis of ratings data. Decision makers often need help, and the least we can do for them and those whose performance they review is to provide valid information and assistance in using it efficiently and accurately. Student ratings can provide some of the information needed for evaluative decisions. The quality of this information should be closely monitored, and research should continue to establish the most effective ways of collecting and presenting it. We owe one another and our students no less than an equivalent effort, to ensure that student-ratings practice is well informed and that evaluation data are properly used.